Finding God's plan for my life

Lemons to Lemonade

Sylvia Matiko
and Pat Moore

Pacific Press® Publishing Association
Nampa, Idaho
Oshawa, Ontario, Canada
www.pacificpress.com

Cover design by Eucaris L. Galicia and Gerald Lee Monks
Inside design by Steve Lanto
Cover photo provided by Sylvia Matiko

ISBN 13: 978-0-8163-2190-2
ISBN 10: 0-8163-2190-6

Additional copies of this book are available by
calling toll free 1-800-765-6955 or by
visiting http://www.adventistbookcenter.com.

07 08 09 10 11 • 5 4 3 2 1

Dedication

In grateful acknowledgment of His tireless pursuit,
this book is dedicated to the One who longs for an
intimate friendship with each of His children.

Contents

Foreword

Every once in a while, I do what's called a lemonade fast. For seven to ten days, all that enters my body is lemonade. I know that sounds like a junk-food fast, because, of course, lemonade is not known to be a nutritious beverage. Ah, but I have a special recipe. No store-bought pink liquid filled with refined sugar is involved. Oh, no! My concoction is composed of twenty ounces of water, two tablespoons of fresh squeezed lemon juice, two tablespoons of grade B maple syrup (which is the stage at which it is most mineral rich but less sweet), and a pinch of cayenne pepper. Shake it up and drink as much as you need to maintain energy and suppress hunger, one twenty-ounce bottle after another all day long. The beverage is far more yummy than it sounds. The taste is superb. But I don't drink it for the taste. The point of the lemonade fast is to give the body a rest and a cleanse while increasing mental energy.

Every time I do this fast, I feel as if my spiritual perceptions become more acute and focused, which is exactly the effect this delightful book has had on me. It's been a kind of spiritual lemonade fast for me. Sylvia and Pat have brought together a tremendously helpful series of insights skillfully communicated in the form of personal testimony. It's a page-turner full of heart—theirs and God's. Chapter by chapter, the reader gets the distinct impression that God is a very real Person who is eager to be involved in our "little" lives, which is the only impression worth having about God. Anything short of that, and this big universe cannot but turn out to be frightening. Pat and Sylvia have raised my awareness of God's love, His care, and His passion for me. Thank you, my dear sisters.

Ty Gibson

Introduction

"Sylvia, are you sitting down?" asked the voice over my cell phone.

It was Easter weekend, and I was on the way to the mall with my sister-in-law and two young nieces.

"Well, Girlfriend, I did it!" my friend, Pat, exclaimed.

"Did what?" I asked.

"I just finished the first chapter of your book!"

"What!" I shrieked. "You did? How? When did you decide to write it?" My excitement and questions drowned out the noisy chaos created by the two little girls in the back seat.

And so began the journey of the book you now hold in your hands. It's the story of my journey—a journey that carried me far away from God—and of the people and means He used to bring me home again. It's the story of God's creative and patient love. It's the story of God's eagerness to teach and to reveal Himself. It's the story of God's ability to use even the most unlikely of us.

I had the honor of presenting the story of this journey at the Kentucky-Tennessee Women's Retreat in the fall of 2003.

In fact, part of the story is the result of preparing for that speaking engagement. Following the retreat, a number of women requested a copy of the material I had shared over that weekend. Through those requests, I sensed God calling me to put the information in a book.

"Lord, I can't do that! You know I am not a writer!" was my answer to His prompts.

Then my friend Pat came to mind. She is a writer; she could tell this story for me. So I asked her to consider putting my story and our shared experiences into written words. She was dubious at first, but agreed to pray about it. One morning she awoke with the opening scenario fixed in her thoughts and realized that perhaps God did want her to have a part in the telling of this story.

Each of our life journeys is unique, and yet we have doubts, fears, and desires in common along the way. I invite you to travel with me, and I hope, as I share my experience, you will discover that God is never far away, that He holds the answers you are seeking, and that He can't wait to show you the passion, joy, and contentment He has planned especially for you!

"I know the plans I have for you," declares the LORD, "plans to prosper you and not to harm you, plans to give you hope and a future."
—*Jeremiah 29:11*

Chapter 1

The Search

I drove slowly into the church parking lot and pulled into the first available space. Instead of getting out and heading for the door, I sat quietly behind the wheel.

This is it, Lord. If it doesn't work this time, I am not going to try again. Three strikes and You're out, I told God.

I really do want this to succeed, don't I? With a plea from my heart, I opened the door and, with much trepidation, walked toward the church entrance. *What will I experience this time?*

Let me introduce myself. My name is Sylvia Matiko, and I am a professional businesswoman. I enjoy people and thrive under pressure. For most of my career, I worked at Ripley Entertainment (yes, the Ripley's Believe It or Not! corporate headquarters) as one of their vice presidents and traveled extensively. I now have my own company and help business owners, CEOs, and other top executives handle their business challenges. The journey to this point in my life has been like a big roller-coaster ride in a theme park, a "five-ticket ride" as we say in the amusement industry! Come along with me for the ride as I share my story.

My mother and father, both of German descent, differed in their religious backgrounds. Before their wedding, my Catholic father requested that his children be raised in the Catholic faith. My mother, a nonpracticing Seventh-day Adventist, agreed. So, as an infant, I was baptized into the Catholic Church, but our family's attendance was sporadic at best. I attended only the Catholic Church until my grandmother came from Germany to visit us in Toronto.

"Milda," she asked my mother, "will you find me a Seventh-day Adventist congregation to attend while I am here? And it needs to be one that speaks German!"

A very strict Seventh-day Adventist, my grandmother would never think of missing Sabbath services.

My mother obliged, phoning around until she found one. Surprisingly, my father encouraged her to take my grandmother to services. But after Oma returned to Germany, my father demanded that our attendance stop. However, my mother continued to attend a Seventh-day Adventist church, taking my brother and me with her.

So began our dual-church controversy. Sometimes we'd attend church on Saturday; sometimes we'd go on Sunday. A few times we attended church both days! Eventually my mother returned to her spiritual roots, a decision causing a great deal of strife in our home. My father was very upset, certain that we were being brainwashed in that Saturday church. I was not surprised at his reaction, but things at home became so tense, I realized this issue had the potential to destroy our family. It really frightened me. I valued my father's opinion, but I was raised to think for myself, to question everything, and to accept nothing at face value. I still tend to be skeptical, sometimes to my detriment. But because of the love of my parents for each other, and because of my mother's trust in God, the tension lessened over time, yet it never completely disappeared.

As the time neared for me to enter my junior year of high school, I was determined to attend Kingsway College, an Adventist school, rather than attending the public high school in our area. I knew getting my father's permission would be almost impossible. He was still concerned about his children being brainwashed.

My mom broached the subject with him but was promptly told "No!"

"Sylvia," she said to me, "just give this idea a rest for a few weeks. Then why don't you talk to him over summer vacation. Because you're his little girl, he will probably at least listen to what you have to say."

The summer holidays progressed, and as the deadline for my application drew near, I knew the time to confront my dad had come.

"Daddy, I need to talk to you." I climbed onto his lap and wrapped my arms around him just as I had as a little girl.

"I don't want to go back to Orangeville High School. I am afraid. Every day someone asks me if I want to buy drugs. Lots of the kids are drinking. My classmates are getting pregnant. And last year one of the kids was murdered. I don't want to be there! In fact at one of the Friday night dances last year, they had policemen stationed at the entrance, and all the other exits were barred with heavy chains. I don't know what might happen if I have to go to school there next year. Please, may I go to Kingsway?"

When he realized how frightened I was about attending Orangeville High, he agreed to take a look at Kingsway College. We made the two-hour drive so that my dad could see the campus. Having a daughter attend a private school was a bit of a status symbol, too, and I was quick to point this out to him. He finally relented, agreeing to let me attend.

It was a hard transition from home to a boarding school, and as a normal teenager—one who questioned everything—my time at Kingsway was not without its moments of crisis. I was rebellious, pushing the limits as far as I could without getting expelled. Even so, those years gave birth to a lot of wonderful friendships that have lasted through the years.

One particular trial was the annual week of prayer. How I hated it! On the outside, I complied, playing in the band and attending the meetings, but when the altar calls were made, I cringed!

It is just emotional manipulation, I rationalized. I wasn't going to succumb to peer pressure and walk down to the front of the chapel. I was not going to let them brainwash me as my father had so often warned.

After Kingsway, it was on to Andrews University. This transition was no easier than the first one. Enduring more rules and regulations and required worship attendance, I couldn't wait to get out of there. My attitude softened a bit when I joined the school's gymnastic team, and although I felt God's tug on my heart, I resisted. After all, wasn't I doing all the right things? I read all the books, I read my Bible, and I took all the required religion classes! But when the week of prayer rolled around and the altar calls were made, I sat there shaking my head at the misguided people following what I was sure was an emotional whim. I was not going to be trapped like that!

After obtaining my business degree from Andrews University, I set out to conquer the world. I was ready to escape the world of Adventists, but God had a different idea! Ironically, I was hired by Crawford Adventist Academy. Does God have a sense of humor, or what! I became the bookkeeper and then school system accountant. But when I was asked to teach an accounting class, I turned down the invitation.

"No way! I am not a teacher!" I stated emphatically.

The school board assured me that certification would be an easy process and begged me to agree. I just couldn't! I knew something they didn't that would be a major complication in acceding to their request. You see, I was not a baptized member of the Seventh-day Adventist Church. It was a step I had never taken. I pretended to be a member, and no one at Crawford had ever asked me that particular question. I was sure I'd be fired if it were known. It was decision time. What was I going to do?

I did what was comfortable and familiar. I ran. I found a job as a controller for an interior-design company.

Phew! That was close, I thought. *No baptism for me!*

During this time I married the man of my dreams. Warren had been raised an Adventist but was not attending church. So, although my church attendance had been erratic, after our marriage, I stopped attending altogether. What did I need church for? Hadn't I already found a husband? Isn't that why all young girls go to church anyway? I was ecstatic to be free, outside the Adventist bubble. The new kind of freedom we found felt wonderful! My husband and I were having the time of our lives.

My brother used to say, "Sylvia, you two are living a beer commercial!" And he was just about right. We were working hard, playing hard, and living only for ourselves. We had it made! No more rules, no more regulations, no more religious hypocrisy! I was so glad to be free of all that. My life in the fast lane had finally begun. I was beginning to live my dream.

Then I was offered a great job working for Ripley's Believe It or Not! as their corporate controller. Soon I was promoted to vice president of finance, then to vice president of franchise operations, which allowed me to travel the world, seeing many wonderful places. I worked long hours seven days a week and got to meet many famous people, such as Jimmy Carter, Margaret Thatcher, George Bush, and Colin Powell. I was rated as one of the few women executives in Canada who broke through that glass ceiling so many women come up against.

When Ripley's moved their corporate headquarters from Toronto, Canada, to Orlando, Florida, we moved with them. We bought a big, beautiful house, and I drove a company car. We were living the "good life"! I had a great salary, furs, jewelry, a fantastic job, and a travel budget. What more could anyone want?

In the Orlando area, I ran into Shawn, a former classmate from my academy days. I think we both enjoyed renewing our friendship.

"Sylvia, how about coming to a women's ministry tea with me at our church?" Shawn asked one day.

"No way!" I told her. "You are not going to get me into a church."

"Oh, come on, it will be fun!" Shawn persisted.

I was very reluctant, but Shawn was lovingly persuasive, and eventually I agreed to attend. You can believe that I was on my guard as I walked into the church, sure that someone would try some arm-twisting—but the tea turned out to be a delightful experience. No one tried to convert me. No one was out to beat me over the head with their religious ideas. I survived stepping back into a church and had to chuckle at myself as I realized all the emotional baggage I was carrying.

I was not about to make church a part of my routine, however; I was enjoying the "good life" too much. For twelve years I had been living this lifestyle, but unfortunately, life in the fast lane does take its toll.

I was the only female executive at Ripley's and felt extra pressure as a result. The guys would get home at six-thirty in the morning after a thirty-hour flight from Asia, and they would be in the office by afternoon. And though my body and mind craved more sleep and relaxation, I forced myself to head into the office too. I was exhausted but would never admit that I was having difficulty keeping up with the guys. Of course, they had wives to do their laundry and the grocery shopping! Warren was a big help, but since I was the wife, I felt those chores were part of my responsibilities. Juggling the demands of a full-time career and home can become overwhelming. I felt the pressure and guilt build up before each trip. I would try to leave prepared meals for my husband, even though he assured me it wasn't necessary. His assurances that he would be fine only added to my feelings of guilt. The internal pressure continued to mount.

Although I was busy and secure in my career, my husband was struggling. Finding a position when we first moved to Orlando was not easy for him. He'd finally taken a job that required well over an hour's commute each way, but the distance soon grew to be more than he wanted to endure. He then found a consulting job requiring a bit of travel, and since I was traveling as well, I thought it was great. But as often happens, the hours he was needed began to decrease, and soon he was working only ten hours a month. So his job search began anew.

I remember one day finding a one-inch-thick folder in our home office that was filled with rejection letters. I was blown away! I could just imagine how this was affecting Warren's self-esteem, especially when people were beginning to tease him about living off of his wife. Though said in jest, I knew the words made him uncomfortable. My concentration on my job didn't help the situation any either.

Warren's job search eventually turned up a job in Salinas, California. By this time, our relationship had become strained due to the stresses we were both under. Warren really wanted to try this job, so we decided he should move to California by himself to give it a trial run. One of the most depressing times I've experienced was when we found an apartment for him and began to furnish it with the essentials. Living in separate households didn't fit with my picture of the good life. Warren and I did still manage to see each other occasionally. Whenever I traveled west, I routed my trip through San Francisco or San Jose so we could get together. And he made it back to Orlando a few weekends too. But the situation was less than ideal.

During this time, I had a regularly scheduled checkup with my physician. Not anticipating anything unusual, I was completely surprised when I received a phone call from his office the following day informing me that my mammogram results were irregular. I would need to schedule some additional testing at the hospital. I was at the office when that call came through, and after hanging up the phone, I remember thinking *What just happened here?*

Since the nurse would give me no details, I promptly called my brother, a radiologist, and asked him what was going on.

"Sylvia, don't worry about it. They probably just need some more films to get a better view. It happens sometimes," he responded.

The technician who examined my breasts the next day was very kind and compassionate, but she kept coming back and repeatedly taking more pictures of my right breast. I was getting more and more nervous by this time and begged her to tell me what she knew.

"You have a lump in your breast," she said, taking my hand and showing me exactly where it was. I could feel it!

"Can this really be happening?" I moaned. I was in shock.

They scheduled me for an ultrasound the following day. My physician would be there to take a look at the mass.

When I got home, I called my brother again and told him the results of the tests done that morning.

"Raymond, they found a lump in my breast."

There was complete silence on the other end of the line. Then realizing my fear, he replied, "The ultrasound is a typical procedure. I am sure they are just wanting to be sure of any irregularities." But I could tell that he was very concerned.

"It's probably nothing!" Raymond added. Then he quoted the percentages of women whose masses turn out to be benign, but I don't remember much of what was said.

When I called my husband in California to tell him I was scheduled for an ultrasound, his response was the same as my brother's—dead silence. I knew that Warren wanted to be there with me, but it was impossible. There was no way he could take time off from his new job, make the necessary travel arrangements, and arrive by the time I was scheduled to be at the hospital.

I didn't try to phone my mother. When I was about ten years old, my mom discovered she had a lump in her breast, and I remember how distraught she was. I was concerned that she would worry herself into a heart attack. I didn't want to tell anyone else. I thought to myself, *I can handle this situation on my own!*

So, the next day, I went off to the hospital—alone. The tests revealed the presence of a mass, but it was benign!

What a sense of relief I felt!

The stress of that experience, however, was stockpiled along with the other stresses in my psyche. Sooner or later, something would have to give.

One day at work shortly after my cancer scare, I began to feel as if I were coming down with the flu. My chest felt heavy, and I couldn't breathe properly. I decided to go to the clinic nearby.

"Mrs. Matiko, there is nothing wrong with you," the doctor informed me after giving me a thorough checkup.

"I suggest that you resolve whatever issues you are struggling with and lessen the stress you are under. Your symptoms are a result of too much stress. You are having an anxiety attack."

What! That's impossible! I am not under too much stress! I told myself.

He just looked at me and said, "I suggest you enroll in a stress reduction and management class." He wrote on my medical chart: Diagnosis: anxiety attack.

No way! They just didn't find what's wrong with me, I thought to myself.

But the anxiety attacks became more frequent. They would happen at the oddest times. I would feel lightheaded, and my breathing would become irregular. My chest would tighten, and I would feel faint. But I refused to accept the possibility that my body might be trying to tell me something.

My mother-in-law was among the first to notice that all was not well. The subtle signs of discontent were visible to her. I was so busy, always on the go, always moving on to the next challenge, that I could not see what she saw. And she picked up on the telltale signs of a growing distance in my marriage.

"Sylvia, if you don't start taking better care of yourself, the next time I see you, it will be in a hospital!" she warned. I was still in denial. I couldn't believe her words.

I did feel a bit disillusioned. I was working hard, and yet the contentment and happiness I expected weren't there. *Why am I knocking myself out, skimping on sleep, working sixteen- to twenty-hour days, seven days a week? Where is it getting me?* I wondered. I felt that something was missing but had no idea what that something could be.

My family, too, began expressing concern about the effects of my hectic lifestyle. "You can't burn the candle at both ends and expect the fire to burn forever!" they admonished.

I didn't know it then, but God was watching and had a plan. To me, religion was still just a means of control, and I wanted nothing to do with religion or the church. God was well aware of my attitude. He gently reminded me of Shawn and the lovely experience I'd had in her church.

Maybe I need to explore religions a bit more, I thought to myself.

I began questioning my own beliefs and started to examine other religions. I realized that there were some answers I didn't have. I read a lot of self-help books, sure that I could make whatever changes were needed.

After all, it just takes self-discipline, I thought to myself. *I have plenty of that. I certainly don't need any outside help, definitely not any help from God.*

However, I felt like a yo-yo, bouncing from one idea to the next. My emotional turmoil and dissatisfaction increased as the distance in my marriage relationship grew, and I felt helpless to stop it.

When I visited Thailand, I delved into Buddhism and discovered some good principles for living. But as my anger and frustration continued to build, I decided there was no God or any "higher being" and declared myself to be an atheist. My mother was horrified! I remember talking with my mother-in-law, asking her to prove there was a God. I'll never forget her response.

"Sylvia," she said, "I can't prove there is a God. But I can tell you that your way leads only to destruction and death, but my beliefs give me great hope!"

She's got a point, I admitted to myself, *one worth consideration.* And a glimmer of hope started to glow in my soul.

I attended church a few times, mostly to see my friend, Shawn, but then I began to attend because I liked her pastor and her church. He did not hammer doctrines from his pulpit, but talked about developing a friendship, a relationship with God. His down-to-earth stories and sermons created a longing in me to know more. In that congregation, I did not feel judged or condemned because of the clothes I wore or because of my lifestyle.

I remember one particular sermon during which the pastor talked about getting angry with God. I had been taught that such behavior was totally unacceptable and irreverent. But he compared it to our occasional anger with our earthly parents. The pastor said, "He's our heavenly Father and already knows how we feel; He wants honest communication and doesn't mind our anger or our questions."

The concept that God wanted honest communication from His children was a startling idea for me. On my way home from that service, I ranted and railed at God for all that I did not understand: *God, I am miserable! Won't You show me how to make the changes in my life that I need to make? There has to be a way, Lord!*

I read more books and attended church whenever I was in town, but God still seemed so distant. I just wasn't making a connection! I was so frustrated and angry.

At one point, I yelled, "God, if You are really up there, help me!"

I tried to go back to church; I tried to stop working on Saturdays. After all, I understood the importance of the Sabbath! But I also realized that if any significant change in my lifestyle was to be made, I would need to leave Ripley's. But that was no easy task. If I lost that identity, where would that leave me? I am a professional businesswoman, and no self-respecting professional is without a five-year plan. If I changed my lifestyle, what would that do to my plans? What would my purpose be? What would my five-year plan look like?

One day, I sat down with my Bible and decided to play Bible roulette. You know the game: Just let the Bible fall open, randomly point to a passage, and then read the verse. I knew that this was not the way to communicate with God and, in fact, had been told not to expect God to work that way, but I was at the end of my rope!

God, if You really do care about me, You can tell me what I need to know, I prayed.

I was not trying to be flippant; I was just so desperate for an answer, so desperate to know His plan for my life. Believe it or not, God answered that plea. The verse my finger touched read, "Commit to the LORD whatever you do, and your plans will succeed" (Proverbs 16:3). The tears ran down my face as I wept. I knew I had to make a decision. Was I going to commit my plans to God or not? Was I going to trust Him or not?

Sitting there, I prayed, *Lord, here's my five-year plan. You're going to have to figure it out! It's now in Your hands.*

I decided that we should sell our luxurious home and that I should resign from Ripley's. Surely that would take care of a majority of the issues facing me. What I didn't know at that time was that God does things on His timetable, not on ours. Our house was on the market for over a year without a single offer! I felt confused and betrayed.

God, I am doing all this because I want to follow You. So why aren't You taking care of this?

I also wanted to get my marriage back into shape, and Warren was not happy all alone in California. The job was not what he expected, and we were miserable without each other. He wanted to come home, and I wanted him home. We needed to work things out together and really give this a try. *For better or for worse*, I remembered. I made those vows, and I decided I was going to do everything I could to keep them.

Warren came home after about four months in California and started the job search again. It was a difficult struggle, and he tried everything from real estate to mortgage brokering, but nothing clicked.

When he found a job that interested him in Nashville, Tennessee, I thought, *This is the answer to my prayer! This is a way for me to get out of Ripley's and make a new start.*

So I made a deal with God. "Lord, I promise that if the house sells and my husband is offered a position, I will begin regular church attendance."

Well, much to my surprise, the house sold very quickly, my husband was offered a job, which he eagerly accepted, and we were on our way to Nashville.

Friend, God is good, isn't He? Even when we try to bargain with Him, making promises and demands we shouldn't, God looks inside our hearts, and He acts from what He sees there.

He already knew just what I needed and where He wanted me to be. He was working out His plan in His time.

Well, I kept my promise. I called the local Adventist conference office and got the addresses of the Adventist churches in the area. I thought I would try the Adventist churches first, and if that didn't work out, I would work through my list of other denominations. Sabbath morning found me in the first of several Adventist churches in Nashville. The greeters were friendly—but that's their job, right? I sat in the back, on the aisle, so I could escape easily if I needed to. No one spoke to me. I felt like a stranger and so out of place! The experience went downhill from there. It was a very traditional service, the sermon filled with religious jargon. It was way over my head, and I was terribly bored. When they sang the closing hymn, I almost bolted out the door.

Nothing's changed here since the 1970s! I thought as I inwardly cringed. I was so disappointed.

My second Sabbath found me at another church, and though the congregation was friendly, it was not a good fit for me either. I was disheartened.

The following Sabbath was my "three strikes and you're out" Sabbath, mentioned earlier in this chapter. You now understand my desperation as I entered those church doors that morning.

Lord, I pleaded, *please let someone take an interest in me. Let someone reach out to me!*

The greeters were there to smile and shake my hand. I again found a seat in the back and on the aisle. The sermon was good. The pastor used stories and examples I could relate to.

I noticed many young people in the congregation. *That's always a good sign,* I thought. The service ended and I rose to leave. No one had spoken to me.

No one here cares about me either, my heart cried. I was almost in tears as I neared the doors when someone grabbed my elbow from behind.

"Hi! Have I seen you here before?"

I thought I was going to faint! *Has God really answered my prayer? Has He sent an angel?*

My "angel" that day was Gail, the associate pastor's wife. She made me feel so welcome and introduced me to lots of people! She invited me to return and also invited me to her women's Bible study group that met during Sabbath School. I was overwhelmed and felt warm inside. I smiled as I realized I had found a church home.

Friend, does God care about you? Does He still answer our prayers? Does He have a plan for your life? Can He take everything, all the lemons we find in our experiences, and make something good happen? Can He truly make lemonade? I am here to tell you, "He surely can!" I pray that as I share the story of my journey, you will find hope growing in your own heart for the changes you want in your own life.

☙❧

Father God,

Thank You for never giving up on us. Thank You for Your passionate pursuit! Please send a human angel into each of our lives who will show us Your love, grace, and mercy. Continue to take our lemons and make lemonade out of them! Thank You, Lord! Amen.

The Lord is my helper; I will not be afraid.
What can man do to me?
—Hebrews 13:6

Chapter 2
The Decision

I was so happy to have found a church home and eagerly drove to Madison Campus Church each Sabbath to attend services. I enjoyed the sermons and became better acquainted with Gail and her husband, Mike. Gail continued to encourage me to come to her Sabbath School class, and I steadfastly refused. The very thought of attending a Sabbath School class sent shivers down my spine. My memories of previous classes were unpleasant, and the thoughts of going through a daily Bible study guide left me with feelings of anger. I associated those classes with pressure for daily study, pressure for performance, and little relevance to my daily life. *Sabbath School is not for me!* I kept telling myself. But Gail met my objections gently, one by one. She told me that the women's Bible study group she led was not using the regular lesson plan. They were studying the Gospel of Matthew. I admitted to being a bit intrigued. Then one Sabbath, I decided to attend the class. For the first time in more than twenty years, I went to Sabbath School.

My experience that Sabbath morning came as a complete surprise. I was welcomed by about a dozen ladies seated around a large table. I found myself enjoying both the study and the discussion. Those present were open and caring, and I was drawn in by their friendliness. I wanted to come back so that I could get to know them better. One young woman had brought a beautiful orchid that morning and, as we were preparing to dismiss, she turned to me and asked me to accept it as a welcome gift. I was so surprised and touched by this kindness that I was speechless. No one had ever done anything like that before for me.

As you might expect, Sabbath School attendance became a regular part of my routine, and I began to learn how to study the Scriptures. Gail is an excellent teacher, and as a result of her guidance and the sharing that took place in that group, my desire to learn and really dig into God's Word increased. I began to read and study those concepts I found difficult to understand. When I had questions I couldn't answer, I'd call Gail and ask her to explain or to point me in the right direction for the answers I was seeking. My understanding of who God is and how He wants me to relate to Him grew as I studied. Eventually, the idea of baptism pushed its way into my thoughts.

Baptism! That act seemed so drastic! Surely it wasn't really necessary for me, was it? Using my newfound knowledge of how to study the Bible, I set out to find all the texts on baptism and prove to myself that baptism was not necessary. *After all,* I told myself, *I've accepted Him in my heart. That's what's really important!* Using my concordance, I searched text after text. Some passages seemed to support my view, but others did not. One principle Gail had stressed over and over in class was that one needed to study all the texts on a given topic in Scripture, examining the context of each one as well as the content. So being a diligent student, I tried to follow those guidelines. What I discovered surprised me. And I knew what I needed to do. Baptism—a public commitment! I was terrified.

Even though I understood that it was a step I needed to make and I had made the decision, I procrastinated. Don't we all do that when faced with a difficult situation? I just couldn't make myself call Gail or Mike to request baptism. It scared me down to my toes!

One day I was talking to Gail on a totally unrelated matter when I felt a very strong impression. I knew it was the Holy Spirit giving me a gentle push, and before I could stop myself, I blurted out the question, "Gail, do you think Mike would baptize me?" Almost before the words were out of my mouth I couldn't believe I'd asked them! But the words had been said, and the next thing I knew, the date was set. Now, it was time to make my decision known to my family.

As I had anticipated, my mother was so happy! My biggest worry was what my father would say. He would be worried about me, wondering if I'd finally succumbed to the "brainwashing" he'd always warned me about. Could I make him understand that I had not lost my ability to think or to choose, but that I had met a God who wanted a relationship with me, who wanted me to take a stand before the world, saying in effect, "I choose to be a member of God's family"? Could I make him understand it was something I felt compelled to do by my growing love for my Creator?

My father's reaction did not surprise me. He argued and entreated me to think about what I was doing. But in the end, my decision stood firm. It was almost like a test for me. I knew that if I could withstand his arguments and criticism, my decision was for real. It was not just an emotional whim.

I then phoned my husband's parents in Canada to tell them. They were so excited and told me they would come to Tennessee for the big event.

That Sabbath morning, June 12, 1999, will always be a special memory. I remember being nervous and anxious to see my family. Even more special was seeing my father walk into the church foyer with my mom. I'd been pleased when he decided to come down with the family for the weekend, but I hadn't expected to see him at church that morning. The tears welled up in my eyes, spilling over as I saw the love I'd always known my dad had for me. He may not have agreed with my decision, but I was still his daughter and he was there for me.

Gail stood with me in the baptismal tank as I made public my acceptance of God's sacrifice for me. And He blessed me as my husband, my family, and the members of our women's Sabbath School class stood as I took this final step. It had taken me almost forty years to make this decision, and I had fought God almost every step of the way.

Ty Gibson wrote a verse that beautifully summarizes my feelings and experience.

> He took me in His human arms,
>   Calming all my fears;
> He loved me with His human heart,
>   I tasted of His tears.
> Resting there upon His chest,
>   Feeling peace, no dread,
> He whispered words I could now bear,
>   "I'm God, the One you've fled."*

I did it. I surrendered. And what I discovered was a freedom and a joy I hadn't known were available. I'd always feared the restrictions but instead found blessings and a love I've only begun to experience. How much had I missed by my years of resistance and rebellion? That's a question that may never be answered. You might surmise that this is the end of my story, that I'd reached my destination. But, dear friend, the journey had just begun.

∾∾

Dear loving Father,

Thank You for inviting me into the waters of baptism and giving me the courage to make the commitment. Father, I pray that if people reading this story still need to make a decision to follow You, that You will wrap Your loving arms around them and show them there is no reason to fear or flee. Assure them that they can indeed rest their heads upon Your chest and feel the heartbeat of a perfect and unconditional love. Amen.

---

*Ty Gibson, *An Endless Falling in Love* (Nampa, Idaho: Pacific Press® Publishing Association, 2003), 70.

"You did not choose me, but I chose you."
—*John 15:16*

The Relationship

Chapter 3

Broken is not a word that brings a warm feeling to our hearts, is it? It usually means time and money for repairs and the inconvenience of doing without. Sometimes, it also means pain and misery. When something is broken, it's useless! Have you ever found yourself feeling broken and useless? Of no value? We have all felt that way at one time or another, and, friend, I want to tell you that God uses those times to reach us, to teach us. Have you noticed that we can often hear His voice more clearly when our world seems to be falling apart? That's what happened to me.

It wasn't until I felt unhappy, faced problems in my marriage, and started to suffer physically that I began to hear God's voice. It wasn't until I was broken that I realized that I needed changes inside where no one can see. It wasn't until I was broken that I began to search for another way. It wasn't until I was broken that God could make Himself real to me. We are hardheaded people, aren't we? How glad I am that God takes those sour, lemony experiences and makes lemonade!

37

It's a process that begins with brokenness and ends in wholeness. The steps are sometimes painful and sometimes joyful. The process doesn't happen overnight, but it does happen. It's a journey.

As I look back on my journey, I can clearly see some transition points in my attitude.

1. I need You to help me.
2. Help me to know You.
3. Help me to love You.
4. Help me to be passionate about only You.

Take a moment to think about these four transition points. Where are you in your journey? Are you stuck in number one or number four? Does number three make any sense to you? What is the Holy Spirit saying to you right now? I know He is speaking. His passion for you is unmistakable! Take a moment to record your impressions. Write them down! And keep listening, because He's not finished talking to you yet!

I finally realized that I needed help, admitted that God does exist, and accepted that He was there to help me. All I had to do was ask! But I had to come to Him in humility and earnestness. Once He calmed me down so that I could listen, I realized how stupid I'd been in fighting Him all those years. Now that I'd accepted His reality and His gift of forgiveness and had surrendered my life and my five-year plan, what was next? I was still insecure in my relationship with Him. I had not yet learned to trust Him fully, and I realized that I didn't really know Him. I wanted to understand more about this God who had touched my heart with His presence. I wanted to understand Jesus better. At this point in my experience, I had head knowledge but little heart knowledge. I could see that God was working in my heart and my life, but I didn't really know Him.

How do I get to know God? I wondered.

How do I get to know anyone? I asked myself. *You spend time together. You ask lots of questions, questions such as . . .*

- Who are You really, God?
- Why do You want to help me? What's in this for You?
- Who is Jesus, really?
- Why can't I hear Your voice?
- What do You want me to do now? Please tell me what to do!
- Is the Bible really true?

How do we find answers to questions such as these? We can't just walk up to God's front door and ring the bell or meet Him for lunch or call Him on the telephone for a chat! I realized that getting to know God was going to involve a different approach. I realized that if I wanted to get to know Him, I needed to spend more time with Him. That meant studying my Bible. So began my daily studies. Each morning I would sit down and research a topic I was having trouble grasping. Sometimes the answers came, and other times they didn't. But I persisted.

Then one morning Andy, a friend from church, phoned. "Sylvia," he asked, "I was wondering if you would be interested in taking the Experiencing God course? Gail told me that you might enjoy it. It's a thirteen-week course, you have studies to do every day, and you have to commit to attending every week. What do you think?"

Thirteen weeks! I thought, *That's a long time!* I wasn't at all sure that this class was something I wanted to take, but the Holy Spirit suggested that this was an invitation I shouldn't refuse. That still, small Voice whispered in my head that maybe God was trying to help me in my quest for answers. So I signed up for the course and began the process of getting better acquainted with my God.

I remember that first study. The Bible verse for day one, week one was, " 'Seek first his kingdom and his righteousness, and all these things will be given to you as well' " (Matthew 6:33).

What in the world did that mean? What are "His kingdom and His righteousness"? There are question marks all over that page in my study guide.

Do you remember my struggle with my five-year plan? "Lord, what do You want me to do with my life?" I questioned.

I soon discovered that the only thing God wants me to do is to seek Him first. Did you hear that? The *only* thing He wants me to do is to seek Him first.

What does that mean? Do I have to stop work? Does He want me to study the Bible eight hours a day?

Can you just imagine the thoughts that were going through my head? Though I didn't fully comprehend what I read, I kept studying.

The workbook went on to teach that God is the Way. There is no detailed roadmap for my life, no five-year plan! My focus needs to be on God, not on my life.

How many times have we heard the phrase "Jesus is the Way"? Before, the phrase was merely a religious slogan, but somehow the Experiencing God course opened my eyes to what that phrase means and how it looks and feels. Suddenly, it was a new concept!

"I am the Way." *Hmm, no map, no plan.* I did not like the sounds of that at all! I was still asking the question, "God, what do You want me to do with my life?" and I was expecting an answer such as, "Well, Sylvia, I like the fact that you have started your own business. Keep at it, and I will help you succeed." That was not the answer I got.

"Seek first the kingdom of God. I want you to do nothing more than to seek Me first. I am the Way."

Talk about frustrating! What about my career? What about my five-year plan? Everywhere I turned, I kept seeing "Seek first His kingdom!" I began to study and pray that God would teach me about this concept. I wrote in my study guide, "Help me to truly understand the meaning of this command, and thank You for bringing it to light."

Each day's Experiencing God study ends with the question, "What does God want you to do in response to today's study?" I wrote down two things:

1. Change my paradigm from "He'll show me my way" to just "Jesus is the Way."
2. Figure out what "seek first His kingdom" really means.

As the journey continued week after week, I could feel God changing my paradigm. I began to realize what a selfish person I was. Over and over, the study kept reminding me that I am not to tell God what I want to do for Him and ask Him to help me. My focus should be on His purposes and plans, not on mine!

Week two was particularly difficult for me. I put an asterisk beside John 8:47. " 'He who belongs to God hears what God says. The reason you do not hear is that you do not belong to God.' "

Wow! That one really burned me. I was angry! *How dare Henry Blackaby* [the author] *say that I don't belong to God!* (Actually, as I learned later, those words are Christ's!) I read on. "The key to *knowing* God's voice is to have an intimate relationship with Him."*

But how? my heart screamed. *There is that "knowing" part again.* Through the days of study, God softened my heart. I realized that I did want to have an intimate relationship with Him. To be honest, I didn't know exactly what that meant, but more important, I realized God wanted to have an intimate relationship with me. I wrote in my study guide, "Help me to enter into a love relationship with You."

You see, God was teaching me about Himself. I was getting to know Him and at the same time sensing how much I needed Him and how much He loved me.

In week three, He showed me that a love relationship with Him is more important than any other single factor in my life. He showed me that I don't need to be doing something for Him to feel fulfilled. I learned that God was pouring His life into mine. He actually initiates that love relationship.

He chose me! The Creator of the universe wants an intimate friendship with me! How can that be? I wondered. *I thought He was just up there being God! But, He wants a love relationship with me!* It was almost too much for me to take in.

That idea really hit me over the head. It was what I call an "aha!" moment. Can you remember when that realization dawned in your heart? Or are you still waiting for that "aha!" moment in your life? Dear friend, He's calling you. He's wooing you. Can you hear Him? He wants nothing more than to show you He loves you with every fiber of His being! That's all! No hidden agenda. No ulterior motive. God's love is perfect! We were created to be loved and to love in return. Amazing! Are you ready to let Him love you? Are you ready to accept deep in your heart that you are chosen?

❧

Father God,

Thank You for always pursuing us and loving us. Thanks for making us curious.

Thanks for allowing us to question You. Help us to always be honest in our quest for understanding. I pray that the readers will feel and experience Your perfect love. Draw them closer to You than ever before so that they will know You are their Papa. Amen.

*Henry T. Blackaby and Claude V. King, *Experiencing God: Knowing and Doing the Will of God,* Workbook edition (Nashville, Tenn.: LifeWay Press, 1990), 37.

"This is eternal life: that they may know you, the only true God, and Jesus Christ, whom you have sent."
— John 17:3

Chapter 4

Experiencing God

The Experiencing God class changed me. The process was slow, often difficult, and sometimes painful. But ever so gently God was transforming my self-centered, selfish heart. I was seeing things differently. I was truly experiencing God! I was beginning to seek Him first. I craved these lessons, these encounters with God. I was so eager that I wanted to read ahead in our studies and find out everything the author had to teach. However, the facilitator for our group warned us to take it only one step at a time, one lesson each day. I was so thirsty for knowledge. I wanted more!

I finished that thirteen-week course and am forever changed. I began with a head knowledge of my Creator and Savior but encountered a very real and very loving Redeemer. He was so much more than I had known or imagined, so much deeper, so alive and vibrant. This was no aloof God. This was a God who wanted to become involved in every activity and decision in my life! I was beginning to *know* Him. And I think I was beginning to love Him. Days would come when I could sense He was working and wanting me to join Him so that I could experience Him in deeper and more intimate ways. I remember one lesson He taught me about "divine interruptions."

The Experiencing God course lays out seven principles:*

1. God is always at work around you.
2. God pursues a continuing love relationship with you that is real and personal.
3. God invites you to become involved in His work.
4. God speaks by the Holy Spirit through the Bible, prayer, circumstances, and the church to reveal Himself, His purposes, and His ways.
5. God's invitation for you to work with Him always leads you to a crisis of belief that requires faith and action.
6. You must make major adjustments in your life as you join God in what He is doing.
7. You come to know God by experience as you obey Him and He accomplishes work through you.

The inviting and obeying part really hit home that day. Because God works on His own timetable and not ours, when He calls, it's not always a convenient time!

I had just gotten home from vacation, and the mail was piled up, laundry needed to be done, and phone calls needed to be returned. And the business tasks were mounting. I was checking my e-mail, and I noticed one from a friend with whom I had worked at Ripley's. We'd recently renewed our acquaintance via the Internet. She had found my e-mail address, and over the past six months we'd caught up with each other's lives.

Her note was general, just asking how everything was going, nothing out of the ordinary. So I headed on to the next letter. I was in a hurry to get through all my business e-mails to be sure there was nothing vital or pressing that needed my immediate attention. But something stopped me. *Send her a quick reply. Now.*

Odd, I thought to myself, *but, OK.* I began typing a response, answering her queries.

"I just got back from vacation . . . busy playing catch-up . . . "

Then I came to her question, "What have you been up to lately?"

What I had been up to was attending a servant-leadership course taught by Ken Blanchard and Phil Hodges. It was a Christian course, and I discovered I was embarrassed to mention it to her. She wouldn't understand, would she? She knew the "old" Sylvia pretty well, but she did not know this "new" Sylvia. Then I was disgusted at myself for feeling embarrassed!

Just like Peter, denying my Lord! I scolded myself.

Was this a "God is at work and He's inviting you to join Him" moment? Maybe it was! Then, from being like Peter, I turned into a Martha. *Lord, You can't possibly be asking me to do this! I have so much other stuff I need to do right now!*

And just like Jesus said to Martha, I heard His reply. *"Sylvia, Sylvia, you are worried and upset about many things"* (see Luke 10:41).

OK! OK! I yelled back in my thoughts. *I will do it, but I don't know what to say. Lord, You are going to have to write this e-mail for me.*

With more than one hundred e-mails awaiting my attention, two weeks' worth of mail to sort through, and phone calls begging for action, I stopped, knelt in my office, and asked Jesus for help. In my heart, I realized this might be an Experiencing God moment.

I did not know my friend's spiritual situation, but I knew that God did. I prayed for His guidance and the right words as I told her about the Christian leadership course I'd just taken. I told her how fortunate I was to meet CEOs in Nashville that operated under Christian values, and I asked her if she'd ever heard of Ken Blanchard.

I prayed as I finished that letter and with much trepidation, sent the message. As the "Your e-mail has been sent" message flashed on my computer screen, I offered another prayer. After only ten minutes, she responded! I was so surprised and very curious to see what she had to say.

"I've heard of Ken Blanchard. I wonder if our company would be interested in his program. They are Christians and recently had someone give a presentation on time management. Are you much into religion, Syl?" she asked.

The question floored me. *Lord, how do I respond to that?* Oh my goodness! What was I going to say now? I didn't want to shove religion down her throat, but I didn't want to continue being a Peter either. So again I got down on my knees and prayed.

Lord, I don't know what You are doing here or what words You need her to hear from me. I have to fully trust You and listen to what You have to say. I am at a loss. Please give me the right words! I don't have any idea how she feels about You, but this has obviously struck a chord with her.

My heart was pounding as I returned to my keyboard to answer her question. "You asked if I was into religion. I am not much into religion per se, I am more into relationship. I do believe there is a God. (Didn't think that way a few years ago!) If He created me, then He has a purpose for me. He knows what's best for me, so I'm still trying to build this ideal relationship with Him. And I am not much into telling people unless they ask. I hate having 'religion' shoved down my throat! For me, it's more about building a relationship with the Guy who made me and trying to figure out life His way. I've proved that I can't 'do life' right; I've made lots of mistakes. So, if there is a better way, one that synchronizes with the Guy who made me, things should flow better, right? I figure if I get that right, the rest will follow. What about you?"

Her response was quick and to the point.

"Re: Religion. I like your theory, Syl. I am really surprised to hear you say that you can't 'do life' right. I would never have expected that from you. It's good to hear you admit it, though. Not many people will. I admit too that I am really into the spiritual side of myself right now. I am trying to find the real me and the real meaning of life. I love learning all this stuff. It makes me realize that life does not end here, there is so much more to learn and live! I like the way you think about this subject! I went to church last year for the first time in my life and I loved it. But I don't go much. Oh, one more thing, just how are you discovering this being in synch with the Man Upstairs? By going to church, or some other way?"

Wow! I was blown away as I read her letter. *Oh Lord, what's going on here?* I prayed as I placed my fingers on the keyboard and began my response.

"The first thing I did to get 'in synch' was to think about who He was and to ask myself 'how do you build a relation-ship with someone, particularly someone who is invisible?' Well, you need to spend time with people if you want to get to know them, so I began to talk to God, asking Him to show me 'whatzup' and admitting that I needed help."

I then shared some of the story of my search and suggested she check out a Christian bookstore. Then I told her about taking the Experiencing God course and the impact it had on me. As I touched the Send Mail key, I could only wonder where this would lead.

We sent a couple more notes that day, and I shared with her a list of books and authors that I'd really found helpful. I sent her some short Bible studies, too, though I don't know whether or not she went through them. That part is not up to me; it's up to her. However, I do know that God used this divine interruption to help another daughter He loved very much draw closer to Him! God used me to help her, and in doing that, He helped me too! During those couple hours, I experienced God's guidance, and afterward, looking back at the events, I was blown away to see what He had done! He knew her heart. He knew exactly what she needed to hear. He knew He wanted to use me. My part was to obey, and when I did, I experienced His love.

Dear friend, I could tell you story after story like this. It is absolutely amazing! You too, can experience God in a very real and tangible way.

I can almost hear you saying to yourself, *That could never happen to me!* That's what I, too, thought a few years ago. But it can happen, and God is eager at the prospect! He can hardly wait to start a relationship with you!

God is alive and well, dear friend! And His Son, Jesus, knows exactly what you are going through, exactly what you are facing. The Holy Spirit wants so much to be your Guide and Coach! If only you will allow Him! Get to know Him, really *know* Him.

So often, we look for formulas, an easy way to reach an end, a step-by-step plan to follow. I am a "type A" personality, largely task oriented and task driven. What I learned through the Experiencing God course was that the Christian life is all about seeking Him first. That's the only task we have. It's so simple, but we have a real knack for making it complicated.

For each of us, seeking may happen in a different way. Each of us is unique and individual. What happened with me was tailor-made for me. What happens in your life will be unique and special for you. The bottom line is that God is eager to create a distinct and personal journey for you. He wants you to *know* Him. He wants you to fall in love with Him. Friend, He is crazy about you! The only thing He wants you to focus on right now is getting to know Him. That's all He's asking. Get to know Him. And when you do, when you begin to see His beauty and love, you will begin to fall in love. Do you *know* God? Do you really love Him?

It's never too late to start, and an intimate relationship like this is too precious to miss!

∂◦⊰

Dearest Father,

Thank You for relentlessly pursuing us. Help us to see You in the small stuff. Keep us alert to those "divine" interruptions we may resent, but that result in such rich blessings if we obey. Please continue to be our Guide and Coach. Help us to always seek You first, realizing the rest will fall into place if we do. Amen.

---

*Henry T. Blackaby and Claude V. King, *Experiencing God: Knowing and Doing the Will of God,* Workbook edition (Nashville, Tenn.: LifeWay Press, 1990), p. 20.

Your attitude should be the same as that of Christ Jesus:
Who being in the very nature God,
did not consider equality with God something to
be grasped,
but made himself nothing,
taking the very nature of a servant,
being made in human likeness.
And being found in appearance as a man,
he humbled himself
and became obedient to death—
even death on a cross!
—Philippians 2:5–8

Chapter 5

The Surprise of Servanthood

"Amelia, have you ever heard of Edward Christoff Philippe Gerard Renaldi?" her grandmother asked.

"No," Mia answered.

"He was the Crown Prince of Genovia," she replied.

"Umm . . . what about him?"

"Edward Christoff Philippe Gerard Renaldi was your father."

"Yeah, sure. My father was the Prince of Genovia. Uh-huh. You're joking!" was Mia's response.

"Why would I joke about something like that?" her grandmother queried.

"No! No . . . 'cause if he is really a prince, then I am . . . ," Mia's shock was evident.

"Exactly!" her grandmother beamed. "You're not just Amelia Thermopolis, you are Amelia Mignonette Thermopolis Renaldi, princess of Genovia!"

"Me? A princess? Shut up!" Mia squealed.[1]

Surprises come in all shapes and sizes. Some bring joy, and others usher in times of pain and sorrow. Some simply add a touch of sparkle to our days, and others change our lives forever. And, as Princess Mia discovers in *The Princess Diaries,* surprises often mean that difficult decisions lie just ahead.

OK, Lord, now what? I asked. *You've started to teach me about watching to see where You are at work. You've started to teach me about divine interruptions. You've started to teach me about always pursuing a love relationship with You. What's next?* My quiet time was filled with questions.

Concluding that more Bible study was in order, I wondered what topic I should dig into next. I admit I felt a bit overwhelmed. The Bible is a huge book filled with lessons, and I had no idea where to begin.

After praying, I headed to a local Christian bookstore, asking God to show me what He wanted me to study. I wandered the bookstore aisles, praying as I walked.

Lord, out of all these books, what's next on Your agenda for me?

I probably spent a good hour looking over the titles on the shelves, reading the back covers of those that piqued my interest, and then returning them to the shelves.

One area of my life that was turning out to be a particularly difficult struggle was figuring out how my vocation fit into God's plan and discovering how He wanted me to join Him. *How do I combine my career with what God wants me to do? Am I in the "right" line of work?* After settling in Nashville, I had started a consulting company that helped small businesses with some of the issues they faced. But I had a gnawing feeling that changes were needed, that the coming months would bring an upheaval. My journal entries were filled with my frustrations over this conflict. *What occupation should I pursue? Do I continue with what I've started? Is this where You are working Lord?* I wasn't getting any answers, so I kept searching. Surely God had the solutions I needed; I just needed to be persistent!

I have always enjoyed reading the books by John Maxwell. I like books on business and am naturally lured to buy books on leadership. So I was drawn to that aisle in the bookstore, but nothing seemed to grab my interest. I headed next for the Bible Study/Small Group Study section, hoping I would come across something there.

Jesus on Leadership: Becoming a Servant Leader. The title seemed to jump off the shelf at me. *What an odd title,* I thought. *I wonder what that could be about. It could be interesting!* The term *servant leader* in the title seemed to be an oxymoron.

Reading the back cover, I noted that the book dealt with leadership, and it promised to address one's vocation. *Wow,* I thought. *This is right up my alley!*

I bought the book and headed home to launch my study on servant leadership. I eagerly began searching the Scriptures to learn about some of the great leaders of the Bible, to discover what qualities made them exceptional leaders.

The more I studied, the more convinced I became this was an area I needed to surrender to God, allowing Him to work on me. I had been taught the typical business perception of leadership: Leadership is authority. There was always a leader with many underlings. The leader had power, was respected, and exerted influence. I recognized that I had been a leader, and I was proud of that fact.

But this new model of leadership was addressing concepts such as humility, service, doing nothing out of selfishness, and looking out for the best of others. These ideas in connection with leadership were completely new to me. The study guide used Jesus as an example of the true servant leader and, through passages in Philippians, showed me that Jesus came to humble Himself as a servant. That was a totally novel way of thinking about leaders. In corporate America, one climbs the corporate ladder to a role of leadership. In the "corporation of the kingdom," one climbs down the ladder into "servanthood." That was a huge paradigm shift to my thinking and the way I had been taught.

Other verses in the Bible supporting that same theme began coming to my attention as I studied.

- " 'Whoever wants to become great among you must be your servant, and whoever wants to be first must be slave of all. For even the Son of Man did not come to be served, but to serve, and to give his life as a ransom for many' " (Mark 10:43–45).
- "Humble yourselves, therefore, under God's mighty hand, that he may lift you up in due time" (1 Peter 5:6).
- "Do nothing out of selfish ambition or vain conceit, but in humility consider others better than yourselves. Each of you should look not only to your own interests, but also to the interests of others" (Philippians 2:3, 4).

The Bible study also gave me some key ideas:

- When you are a servant leader, you are a steward or manager of God's grace in your life.
- You are to use all God gives you to serve others.
- God gifted you for His glory, not your gain. God gifted you to build His church, not your ego.

- God uses every moment—from your birth and family of origin to the events of today—to mold you into a servant leader for His purposes.
- Servant leaders can risk serving others because they trust that God is in control of their lives.
- Servant leaders give up personal rights to find greatness in service to others. Without God-centered certainty, you have no choice but to protect your ego and defend your rights. Only when you trust God with absolute control of your life can you risk losing yourself in service to others.[2]

I could not believe what I was reading! It was truly an "aha!" moment for me. I had been missing this truth my entire life, yet Jesus was the True Model of it. How could I not have seen it?

Then it hit me right between the eyes. I realized that I had been a "self-serving" leader, not a "servant leader"—and that realization hurt! I bowed my head, praising God for showing me this ugliness deep within me. I prayed right then that God would humble me and make me His servant leader.

Another "aha!" moment occurred when I read and began to understand this passage found in Colossians: "Whatever you do, work at it with all your heart, as working for the Lord, not for men. . . . It is the Lord Christ you are serving" (Colossians 3:23, 24).

Insight from this passage helped me understand clearly that it doesn't matter what my career is, as long as I work hard as if working for the Lord. It is an attitude and has nothing to do with vocation. God didn't call me into a special career or vocation! He has called me into a love relationship with Him—

plain and simple. After that day, I no longer separated "God's calling" from "my career." God can use anybody in any job to do His will. God's calling is always to live your life for Him in every area. God may use your vocation to enhance His call on your life. He decides when and how your calling to follow Him blends with your vocation.

I had been sharing my newfound insights with my friend Andy when he told me about another book he thought I'd enjoy, *Leadership by the Book* by Ken Blanchard, along with Phil Hodges and Bill Hybels.[3]

"Sylvia, if you like this leadership stuff, this is a good book, and it goes into servant leadership too," Andy shared.

I was familiar with some of Ken Blanchard's material and, in fact, had used some of his principles in my consulting practice. I thought of him as a "management guru." He had "made it big" as the author of the *Leadership and the One Minute Manager*, a book outlining simple principles that, when applied, make a great manager. Needless to say, I was intrigued and purchased *Leadership by the Book*.

In typical Blanchard parable style, the book takes the reader through the struggles of business, but in the most fascinating way—the servant-leadership way! I could hardly believe what I was reading: a secular author broaching this subject matter, using Jesus' example as a servant to teach how "to do" business by the book! I devoured it in just a few sittings. (For me, that's phenomenal; reading is not my passion!)

I was so impressed with the contents of the book that I did something I'd never done before. I decided to write a letter to the authors. The book included the information that Phil Hodges and Ken Blanchard had set up a company called The

Center for Faithwalk Leadership, and they were offering seminars based on the material presented in the book. I wanted to find out if any seminars were planned for the Nashville area. So, I wrote to Phil and Ken, telling them how impressed I was with their book, how it had helped me to make some needed changes, and that I'd be interested in attending one of their seminars. I mailed the letter, never really expecting a response.

About four weeks later, I was deep into a client meeting when the phone rang.

"Hi, this is Phil Hodges from The Center for Faithwalk Leadership. Is Sylvia there?"

Now, I am rarely speechless, but I didn't know what to say or how to respond. I uttered a stunned and polite, "Yes, this is Sylvia."

Phil told me how much they had appreciated my letter. And he did so in such a humble way that I could sense the presence of Jesus in his heart. His attitude somehow traveled over the telephone line.

He told me that there was going to be a seminar in Tennessee, close to Nashville, in Brentwood. He wasn't sure how close that was to me, but he wanted me to know what was planned.

That was the second shock. Brentwood is just down the road from my home in Franklin. In fact, until just recently, we'd lived in Brentwood!

I got so excited. "That's exactly where I live! I'd love to come. How do I sign up?" I questioned.

Phil went on to tell me that Brentwood Baptist Church was hosting the seminar and gave me the phone number of the people I should contact. Then we chatted a bit more.

Here was an author of a book, calling little ol' me! No secretary connecting me, no "air" about him. Phil Hodges, humble and loving, who thought of himself as no more than a servant of Christ who was talking to a daughter of Christ. It was as simple as that.

As I hung up the phone, my client looked at me in the strangest way. "What was that all about?" he asked. I smiled and gave him a polite answer, but inside, I was jumping for joy! I was so excited about the possibilities of meeting Ken and Phil and participating in the seminar.

The very next day, I called the local seminar planners. They had just started putting together a committee to help bring the seminar to this area and wanted to know if I would be willing to help out. By the end of the conversation, I was part of the committee to bring the Faithwalk leadership seminar to Nashville. I was blown away!

Lord, what path do You have me on? I exclaimed. Little did I realize what was just around the corner!

I felt honored to be on the committee and honored to participate in this seminar. It was life changing for me. Not only was it wonderful to meet Phil and Ken in person, but I met numerous Christian businessmen and businesswomen from Tennessee. I had no idea there were so many CEOs of Nashville companies who were dedicated Christian servants. It was a very humbling experience.

The material presented will forever impact my life, my leadership, and my desire to be a servant of Christ. Thank you to Ken and Phil for allowing me to be a part of this. And it all started with the "What now?" question, God leading me to a study on servant leadership, Andy suggesting that I read *Leadership by the Book,* followed by my writing a letter to Phil Hodges and Ken Blanchard and attending their seminar in Nashville.

But this part of my journey was not over. The Lord still had things for me to learn. A few months later, I was privileged to be invited to another leadership conference simulcast through Willow Creek Church, and the speaker was Bill Hybels, one of the three authors of *Leadership by the Book.* God used all three authors of that book in the space of just a few months to help me learn about His plans. Does God have a sense of timing? Do we have a God who is interested in our personal journeys? We certainly do!

He's not just up there in heaven somewhere, doing His thing. He's using our preferences, our passions, our interests to draw us closer and closer to Him.

I had previously thought that my business life was separate from my spiritual life, that career and calling were two separate things. My journey revealed that I was wrong. Jesus knows just how much I love the business world! After all, He is the One that put that desire in my heart. And He showed me that He can use "business" to accomplish His work. It wasn't necessary for me to change careers; I just needed an attitude adjustment, so to speak. I needed to change from being a self-serving leader to becoming a servant leader. Implementing the servant-leader philosophy was a huge learning curve for me, but over that year, my heavenly Father put the pieces of the puzzle together. I have to chuckle when I look back and see His handiwork in my life. He had the entire puzzle already worked out according to His will. What a Creator we serve!

How can this God of amazing love be so interested and take such delight in customizing an experience for Sylvia Matiko? That thought just blows my mind. He is interested in the little things. He will customize a journey especially for you too. He is doing it right now! You may not recognize it yet, but later, when you look back and connect the dots, you will see His hand in even the small stuff and recognize His intervention.

ఈాళ

To my dearest Father, the best "Puzzle Maker" in the universe,

Thank You for putting the small pieces together just for me. Thank You for teaching me that I was a self-serving leader and not a servant leader. My prayer for all those reading this chapter is that they too will have an "aha!" moment ordained by You, a piece in their personalized puzzle. Thank You for being interested in the small things and for helping us to connect the dots, revealing a picture that, before, only You could see. Amen.

1. *The Princess Diaries,* Walt Disney Pictures.

2. C. Gene Wilkes, *Jesus on Leadership: Becoming a Servant Leader* (Nashville, Tenn.: LifeWay Press, 1996).

3. Kenneth Blanchard, Bill Hybels, and Phil Hodges, *Leadership by the Book: Tools to Transform Your Workplace* (Colorado Springs, Colo.: WaterBrook Press, 1999).

The Lord is good to those whose hope is in him,
to the one who seeks him;
it is good to wait quietly
for the salvation of the Lord. . . .
Let him sit alone in silence,
for the Lord has laid it on him.
—Lamentations 3:25, 26, 28

Chapter 6

Listening

"Did you hear anything I said?"

How many times have you heard those words? How many times have you asked that question? How frustrating to be ignored, to be tuned out! You've been imparting some great important information to your spouse, your child, a co-worker, or a friend when you realize that every word you've spoken has gone in one ear and out the other!

Listening is a gift we give to those who want to communicate with us. It says to them, "You are important! I value your opinion! What you say matters to me!" When we truly listen, we focus all our thoughts and senses on the person speaking and the message being imparted. It's a totally engaging process. It's easiest to listen when all around you is quiet. It's easier to concentrate when there is nothing to distract you.

You may be thinking, "How does this relate to Sylvia's spiritual journey?"

Well, dear friend, I want to share with you a precious discovery. It's called a variety of things: listening, solitude, practicing His presence. But whatever you call it, it is a necessary part of learning to know God. It's listening for His voice, concentrating and focusing on Him.

"Wait a minute!" you might be saying. "Do you mean to tell me that you actually hear a voice speaking to you? This is getting a bit too weird for me!"

Hang on a minute, friend! I am not suggesting you will hear audible voices! But if you take the time to listen, to block out the distractions, the clamor of everyday activities, you will be able to hear the still, small Voice that whispers in your soul. As I practice listening, I am learning to recognize and hear that Voice more often.

Philip Yancey, in *Reaching for the Invisible God*, described an experience he had: " 'Exactly how did God speak?' you may ask. I never heard an audible voice or saw a vision. Admittedly, these insights did not come from outer space; they were inside me all along, a form of spiritual self-awareness. But here is the point: until I took the time to extract myself from the daily routine and commit to long periods of silence, I missed hearing that internal voice. Although God may have been speaking all along, until I opened my ears it made little difference in my life."[1]

Inside of you that still, small Voice speaks too. The problem is that with all the noise around us, we've lost our ability to hear it! Or the message becomes distorted by all the other stuff we've got going on.

One of my favorite people, Mother Teresa, put it this way, "In the silence of the heart, God speaks. If you face God in prayer and silence, God will speak to you. Then you will know that you are nothing. It is only when you realize your nothingness, your emptiness, that God can fill you with Himself. Souls of prayer are souls of silence."[2]

I once explained it to a friend like this: It's a bit like looking for a station on a transistor radio. When we are in the process of finding it and tuning the radio, we hear all sorts of squeals, squeaks, and static. To find the right station takes a bit of fine tuning; eventually it comes in and fades out again. The closer you come to the right frequency, the clearer it gets, until you hear it in stereo! Get the picture? It's time to tune your radio to God's station!

"How in the world do I do that?" you ask. "How do I get in tune with God?"

It involves one of the forgotten disciplines and perhaps the hardest discipline to master. Bible study and prayer—these are familiar; we know how to do those. But solitude? Listening? Who understands how to do that and who has the time for it? Yet, the Bible commands, " 'Be still, and know that I am God' " (Psalm 46:10). How often do we follow that command?

For people like me, it's incredibly difficult to do. I can't sit still! My husband just laughs at me. I'll come and snuggle with him on the sofa, and within ten minutes, I'm up again. I just can't be still! And I have such a hard time unwinding. My husband used to joke that when we'd vacation at the beach, I'd take my briefcase with me and it would be Wednesday before I could leave it alone! He's right! For me, it takes real effort to "be still"! But now, I have come to crave times of stillness.

Let me explain a little how this works, because to begin with, I had it all wrong. I thought solitude meant being alone with God when you are praying or studying the Bible. But then I found out that it means to stop praying, stop studying, stop reading—and listen! That was the difficult part for me! As you can imagine, since I am a people person, I love to talk. Think about it. When you pray, who is usually doing the talking? You are! Well, practicing solitude means that you don't say anything; you just listen.

At the Ken Blanchard servant leadership seminar I attended, he had us do what was for me an awkward exercise. Our assignment was to go outside for one hour, somewhere on the college campus, and just listen. I thought the man was asking the impossible! How was I ever going to remain quiet for one hour! How could I quiet my thoughts? He advised us to pray our wandering thoughts away whenever they threatened to take over the silence.

Well, that hour came and went, and honestly, I felt more than a little frustrated. I didn't "hear" anything. Nevertheless, I decided to try it again in the future. Now I realize that I had never exercised that part of my brain, that part of my spiritual side! So remember, it takes time and practice to get "in tune" with Him.

Now, I cherish the times of solitude and try to practice daily. After I pray and study each morning, I just sit and listen. I've had some amazing experiences doing this. He has brought to mind some texts that I never knew existed, and when I opened my Bible to them, "Bingo!" it was exactly what I needed to hear.

Quite often I'll get an impression that I need to e-mail or phone a friend. I can't tell you how many times the response has been, "Sylvia, hearing from you was just what I needed!" I would have missed out on those beautiful gifts if I hadn't taken the time to listen.

My friend, Pat, had an interesting experience. She was in the process of moving to Hendersonville, North Carolina, after twenty-two years in Nashville, Tennessee, and was having a very difficult time adjusting to the reality of this move.

"Pat, have you taken the time to listen for God's voice?" I asked her.

"No," she replied.

"Are you home alone?" I asked. "Is your husband working tonight? If he is, why don't you take time right now to listen?"

"To be honest, Sylvia, I'm scared to do that! What if I don't hear anything? What if I don't like what He has to say?"

"Pat, just give it a try. Call me afterward and let me know how it went," I encouraged her.

She went out onto her back porch and sat down, watching the dusk deepen. At first she felt silly, sitting out there listening to nothing. All she heard were traffic noises and an airplane overhead. But Pat persisted. As her soul quieted and she asked God to help her listen, she heard a still, small Voice speaking in her heart.

"What do you hear?" it asked. She closed her eyes, listening intently.

I hear the insects, especially the crickets, she answered.

"What are they doing?" was the next question to pop into her head.

Singing! she replied.

"Why?" was the responding question. She had to think about the answer to that question.

Because that's what God created them to do! she exclaimed. As she sat there listening to the night chorus, she realized that she too was created for singing praises to God. She'd been focusing on herself, on the loss of friends and home, and not on her Creator. When we focus on Him, the problems we face somehow become less important. We realize that God is in control and that if we truly trust and know Him, we will be safe and content wherever we are.[3] "When every other voice is hushed, and in quietness we wait before Him, the silence of the soul makes more distinct the voice of God. He bids us, 'Be still, and know that I am God.' Ps. 46:10. Here alone can true rest be found."[4]

You may be thinking that your life is too hectic, that you have too many responsibilities to take time for a spiritual retreat. Or you don't have the resources to make such a time a reality. But if you really desire to know God more deeply, you will make the effort. It doesn't have to be an entire weekend away from family responsibilities and work, although at some point, you may wish to do that. It doesn't mean that you must travel to a monastery or resort to be alone. You can find a quiet moment almost anywhere. Richard Foster, in *Celebration of Discipline*, describes it as "a portable sanctuary of the heart."[5] You may find a place of quiet serenity in the corner of your backyard or a room in your home. You can retreat to a nearby park or walk the streets of your neighborhood. Catherine of Siena was inspired with "the thought of making a chapel in her heart where she could retire mentally and, amid external distractions, enjoy internal solitude. And later, when the world troubled her, she was in no way disquieted, saying that she could always retire into the closet of her heart and seek consolation with her Heavenly Spouse."[6]

"I need to make sure I have a rhythm that includes solitude," writes noted Christian author and pastor John Ortberg. "I have to schedule solitude, write it in the calendar, and protect it fiercely. Sometimes mine are brief periods of solitude; an hour at a nearby forest preserve. Sometimes they are longer—a half-day or a day. But my days for solitude never volunteer. They have to be drafted."[7]

"The Christian life should have a rhythm—doing and resting, speaking and listening, giving and receiving. The life of Jesus illustrates that perfect rhythm. The scriptures indicate that Jesus *worked* at getting alone, just as He worked at serving and teaching."[8]

70

All it takes is a willingness and desire to listen for God's voice in your own heart. He will help you find the time and the space to meet with Him. Friend, are you ready for some solitude? Are you willing to listen? Be prepared; it takes practice. The rewards, however, will astound you!

❧

Dear heavenly Father,

Create in us a yearning to hear Your voice. Increase our desire for the stillness that can be found only in Your presence. Quiet the busyness of our days. Instill in our hearts a craving for solitude and silence. Amen.

1. Philip Yancey, *Reaching for the Invisible God* (Grand Rapids, Mich.: Zondervan Publishing House, 2000), 179.

2. Mother Teresa, *In the Heart of the World* (Novato, Calif.: New World Library, 1997), 19.

3. Pat Moore, "The Cricket's Song," *Women of Spirit*, (September/October 2003), 11.

4. Ellen G. White, *The Desire of Ages* (Nampa, Idaho: Pacific Press® Publishing Association, 1940), 363.

5. Richard Foster, *Celebration of Discipline* (San Francisco: HarperCollins Publishing, 1998), 97.

6. Frances DeSales (1567–1622) "An Introduction to a Devout Life," *Discipleship Journal* 10 (March/April 1995).

7. John Ortberg, "The Unending Tension," *Christianity Today International/Leadership Journal*, (June 10, 2003).

8. Jean Fleming, "Marrying Service and Solitude," *Discipleship Journal* 29 (September 1985).

" 'Love the Lord your God with all your heart and
with all your soul and with all your mind.' "
—Matthew 22:37

Chapter 7

The Command

Love. For most of us, it is the first thing we experience. We don't recognize what it is, but we enjoy the warmth and security that surrounds us as we are cradled in our mother's arms. We respond to her look and touch. It allows us to grow and frees us to begin exploring the world around us. Love is a basic human need, one that holds in its grip the secret to our happiness and contentment. We were created to be loved and to love in return.

A verse in Matthew troubled me when I first read it. " ' "Love the Lord your God with all your heart and with all your soul and with all your mind" ' " (Matthew 22:37).

How in the world do I do that? I asked myself. The more I struggled with that question, the more I realized that I loved many things in my life more than I loved God. Yet He commands us to love Him with all that we are. What does that kind of love look like? What does it feel like? How do I love like that?

I had no answers. No matter how hard I tried, I could not manufacture it. I didn't even know where to begin! The answer came in a most unexpected manner and place.

73

The phone rang.

"Hi, Sylvia! I need to ask you something, and I don't want you to answer right away." Gail's voice sounded excited.

Oh, my dear friend, what are you wanting? I thought. Gail was the women's ministry leader for the Kentucky-Tennessee Conference of Seventh-day Adventists and as such is always involved in one project or another. Her enthusiasm is contagious, and she often drafts her friends to help whenever she can.

"OK, I'm listening," I replied hesitantly.

"Our speaker for the fall women's retreat somehow double-booked her time and will not be able to speak in October," Gail began. "We found out just a few days ago, and I have been praying that God would show me whom else I should ask. Your name keeps coming to mind! I asked a few others what they thought of that idea, and they were very enthusiastic. Would you consider being the speaker for our fall women's retreat?" she asked. "I know that the women would love to hear your testimony, and you would do a wonderful job!"

"What!?" I responded. "You've got to be joking! No way!"

"Sylvia, you have a phenomenal personal story, and I know that you could do this. I don't want you to give me an answer right now. Promise me you will think about it and pray about it?"

Gail's request left me stunned! Surely she was kidding. This just had to be some kind of joke. But from the tone of her voice, I knew the request was for real. I was shaking in my boots at the mere thought of being the retreat speaker!

"Gail, I can't promise anything, but I will pray about it and try to have an answer for you in a week. OK?"

As I hung up the phone, I could feel my heart pounding. *Oh, Gail, what are you getting me into now?* I asked myself.

In the course of my business, I'd spoken many times before large groups, and I'd given my testimony several times in churches, but I'd never before presented a series of personal, spiritual talks. And speaking to a large group of women somewhat intimidated me. I was used to dealing with men in my daily business and so was more comfortable conversing with them. This would be two groups of more than 250 women! I was terrified! In the business arena, I was sure of my message and the material to be presented. In this instance, I was lost. Talk about a need for prayer!

Who am I to talk to these women? I asked myself. I came up with a list of reasons I was not the right individual to be speaking.

1. I am not spiritually mature; I still have so much to learn, so much growing to do!
2. I have so many bad habits that I yet need to overcome. I am no different or better than these women. Why should they listen to me?
3. How can I relate to those who are mothers and understand the stresses they face?

Driving along Interstate 40 to Greenville, Tennessee, to visit family, I was thinking about Gail's request. The reasons I was not the right person for this job just kept circling in my brain. It would be so much easier to just say no! But was that the response God wanted from me?

Oh, Lord, please show me what You want me to do! I pleaded.

Chapter 2 of Philippians pushed its way into my thoughts. I knew the essence of what that text said, but couldn't remember the exact words. Suddenly, I knew that I had to look it up right then. I pulled off the freeway at the next exit. Using a small Bible I carry in my purse, I found the passage I needed, Philippians 2:5–7:

Your attitude should be the same as that of Christ Jesus:

Who, being in very nature God,
    did not consider equality with God some
        thing to be grasped,
but made himself nothing,
    taking the very nature of a servant,
    being made in human likeness.

The word *servant* really seemed to hit home. Presenting the concepts of servant leadership in the business arena had become a passion for me. Now, God was asking me to be His servant. I understood at that moment that He was asking me to accept the challenge Gail had offered; He wanted me to say yes! As I talked with Him about my fears, I heard His voice in my heart telling me that if I agreed to do this, one result would be an unbelievable experience and a deepening of our relationship. How could I refuse an invitation like that?

My lack of spiritual maturity and my fear of not being able to relate loomed large on the horizons of my confidence. Then I realized that no one is perfect and that it was not going to be *me* relating to these women. I would have to let God use me; relating to them would be His responsibility. This weekend would not be about me; it would be about Him! What an awesome responsibility! I felt God calling me to respond to this invitation, but other than my testimony, I was unsure what He wanted me to say.

As I contemplated this task, I understood that in order to prepare, I needed to spend some quality time with the Lord in solitude and silence. I knew I needed to listen and obey, to spend time allowing God to clean me up. When my dear friend Pat heard about the task facing me and my need for a spiritual retreat, she offered her family's lake house for a week. Nestled in the mountains of South Carolina on Lake Keowee, it is a beautiful home in a quietly serene setting. It was the perfect answer to my need. I knew that if I gave the Lord a chance and listened, I would hear Him speak there. Away from the distractions and noise of my everyday world, I would recognize His voice.

Pat is my spiritual sister, a friend as dear to me as Jonathan was to David. We have shared many of the same experiences and frustrations, often finding ourselves on the same spiritual path, enabling us to encourage each other in a remarkable way. It has been amazing! Jesus knows He can use Pat to help me along the way, and vice versa. You see, she is a friend that I can trust with my life. I can share with her my inmost secrets and fears, and she doesn't think any less of me. She loves me anyway—unconditionally. And I certainly needed her that week!

Mornings during our stay there were very special. We would awaken early while there was a stillness in the air. Our first morning we grabbed our Bibles and journals and headed down to the lakeshore to pray. After spending some time alone, we sat together at a table, and I told her of my fears and worries concerning the upcoming speaking engagement.

"Pat, I am so frightened about my speaking appointment!" I admitted.

Pat listened thoughtfully to the reasons for my fears. Then she said, "Sylvia, I read a text this past week that is just perfect for you! 'The LORD himself goes before you and will be with you; he will never leave you nor forsake you. Do not be afraid; do not be discouraged' [Deuteronomy 31:8]."

My eyes filled with tears as I realized that God was indeed in charge. That verse seemed tailor-made for me in this situation, and those words seemed to set the tone for the remainder of the week.

"Pat, I know that God has something very special in store for us this week. He is going to reveal Himself, and we are going to experience something special. I just know it!" I told her.

We were both encouraged as we prayed together for God's presence and for each other's needs. I was the one with the most needs that week, and Pat seemed to understand that and was there for me. She was blessed with a true servant's heart, unselfishly giving herself up for me, and before the week ended, God rewarded her for it.

I told her about my struggle to love God with all my heart and that I didn't feel I was passionate enough about God. Again, we were on the same journey, and she could relate to my frustrations.

"That verse has really been hard for me too," she confessed, "only from a slightly different angle. When I think about what I love most, my kids come to mind. If I am really honest with myself, I'd have to admit that my love for them is stronger than my love for God!

"And then there's that text in Matthew," she continued. " ' "Anyone who loves his father or mother more than me is not worthy of me; anyone who loves his son or daughter more than me is not worthy of me; and anyone who does not take his cross and follow me is not worthy of me" ' [Matthew 10:37, 38].

"How do I respond to that? Does it mean that God wants me to love my son and daughter less? I just don't see how I can do that!" she exclaimed.

What was God trying to tell her? What did He want? It was an issue she'd been striving to understand for months. Her desire was to have a deeper walk with God, but this command had stopped her in her tracks. She remained baffled.

She had been reading a book by Henry Blackaby, *Chosen to Be God's Prophet*,[1] which is a study of Samuel, and interestingly enough, that book led her to Deuteronomy, where she noted the command to love God with all one's heart is given again and again. As she pointed them out to me, I was surprised. I'd never noticed how many times that concept was repeated. I was amazed that Pat and I were on the same path once again. Her fears and concerns were somewhat different from mine, but the core issue was the same.

In my case, it was my business. I am passionate about my business. I love the time spent and the challenge it presents. I love what I do! Does my relationship with God elicit those same responses? Does it pull the same strings in my heart? I felt like I was failing somehow because I knew I cared more about my business than I did about my God. Did that mean that I should give up my business? What did God want from me? Just as Pat struggled with loving her children more than she loves God, I struggled with loving my business more than I love God.

One morning I'd slept in a bit, and when I walked outside on the deck, Pat was sitting at the table with tears coursing down her face. I sat down with her as she shared a text that forever changed my way of thinking.

She'd again been reading in Deuteronomy and came across this: "The LORD your God will circumcise your hearts and the hearts of your descendants, so that you may love him with all your heart and with all your soul, and live" (Deuteronomy 30:6).

"God does not want me to love my children less," she shared. "My love for them is a gift! Love itself is a gift! So loving Him with all my heart would also be a gift! If God wants me to love Him more, and He has said He does, then He will create that kind of love in my heart. I don't have to try to manufacture or force it!"

You know how you begin to think that there is something wrong with you; that you are not doing something right; that you need to do something more? That's the way I felt when I tried to love God with all my heart. Well, dear friend, this is one of Satan's big deceptions! He wants you to think that *you* have to do it. Deuteronomy 30:6 clearly says that it's not up to you! It says God will do the necessary heart surgery. It's God's action, not yours! It's not up to you to love Him with all your heart; it's up to Him to circumcise your heart and fill it with His love! That was a major "aha!" moment for me. Pat and I joined hands and prayed that God would circumcise our hearts completely and continue to reveal Himself to us. It was a moment forever etched in our memories.

Pat is an avid reader, and she came to the lake equipped. The book she was currently reading was *David: A Heart Like His* by Larry Lichtenwalter.[2] She sensed that I needed to read the book while I was there and so, even though she was looking forward to finishing it, she loaned it to me. I am not the reader my friend is, but recognizing Pat's sacrifice, I opened the book and began to read. At first I had difficulty getting into it, but I persevered. Soon I couldn't put the book down! God used that book to invite me to a more intimate relationship with Him. He was inviting me to develop a heart like His.

Lord, can this be? Do You want to have that kind of relation-ship with me? My heart was overwhelmed at the very idea! I knew in my heart that God wanted to have a friendship with me like the one He had with David. Do you remember my certainty that God had something special in store for me in the process of preparing for this retreat? Well, He keeps His word!

During the next few days, God began revealing to me a facet of His character that I'd known intellectually but never completely understood. Love! He loves me! Totally, completely, and passionately! How or why, I don't understand, but His love seemed to surround me. Suddenly I knew what message He wanted me to give the women attending the retreat! He loves them! An all-out, no-holds-barred love! Passionate, complete, perfect! Nothing is more important! I became so excited. God had listened to my questions and given me answers. He truly is a loving God! But now I had more questions: What does that concept of love involve? How does it feel to experience God's love? Does it really change a life? Had I really let it change mine? How could I present God's love in a way that would touch the hearts of others?

Throughout those days at the lake house, I invited God to make whatever changes were needed in my heart, to take self and ego out of the picture so that His words and His love alone would be able to flow through me as I spoke at the re-treat. And I could feel His presence. I could sense His work in my heart. Hour by hour, day by day, He revealed what heart transformations were necessary as I allowed Him to "operate" on my soul.

Have I arrived? Are my life and character perfect? Not by a long shot! But moment by moment, as I invite God to become involved in my daily life, He's opening my eyes, showing me where I need the heart-circumcision process. And if I accept and agree, He begins to alter my way of thinking. I can sense those changes.

Friend, do you love God with all your heart? Is your relationship with Him the most important one in your life? Do you know Him? Do you want to? Have you experienced His love for you? Oh how He yearns to reveal Himself to you! He loves you so! He wants to circumcise your heart so that you can love Him with all your being. He's aching to be asked! He is longing to perform heart surgery, creating in you that wonderful love. Take a moment right now to invite His loving scalpel to make the needed changes. Though the process might involve some pain, the outcome will be a heart overflowing with joy and passion!

Knowing God, discovering the depth and breadth of His love, is a never-ending journey. In the coming weeks, God had more to say, more to reveal about Himself. Are you ready? Hang on; this five-ticket ride is not yet over!

༺༒༻

Father God,

Thank You for revealing to us that our heart's circumcision is in Your hands. Please take Your divine scalpel and remove all that hinders our relationship. Help us to discover anew the depth and breadth of Your love. Amen.

1. Henry Blackaby, *Chosen to Be God's Prophet* (Nashville, Tenn.: Nelson Books, 2003).

2. Larry Lichtenwalter, *David: A Heart Like His* (Hagerstown, Md.: Review and Herald® Publishing Association, 2003).

You are standing here in order to enter into
a covenant with the LORD your God.
—*Deuteronomy 29:12*

Chapter 8

A Call to Covenant

Hello reader! Though we've not been formally introduced, we've met in the preceding pages of this book. My name is Pat Moore, and Sylvia has asked me to share what, for me, was an extraordinary experience that began that week at the lake. As you may remember, Sylvia said that she was sure that we were going to hear God speak and that she was so glad I was there with her! Well, to be honest, I did not really see any need for my presence or how I would be able to help with the task facing her. I was not expecting any big revelations; I was expecting only the joy of spending time with my spiritual sister! However, getting away from the everyday chores that make up much of our lives does sometimes allow exceptional moments to break through. And that's what happened for both my friend and me.

The third morning at our secluded hideaway I awoke early, eager to see what this day might hold. As I came down the stairs, I was greeted by silence and realized that Sylvia was still sleeping. I moved quietly around the kitchen getting something to drink, then grabbed my Bible and my journal and tiptoed out onto the deck. I wanted to just sit there, soaking up the early morning calmness and enjoying the beauty of the lake. The sun was illuminating the trees on the opposite shoreline, and I watched a kingfisher land on the corner of the boat dock. Occasionally a fish would jump, sending ripples swimming toward the shore. I love communing in this spot!

As I prepared to open my Bible, I asked God to lead me to whatever I needed this day. Usually, I'm a bit more systematic in my devotional time, but this morning I did not know where to begin reading, so I prayed for His guidance. I felt impressed to open to Deuteronomy again. The way God was using this part of Scripture to reveal Himself to me was nothing short of astounding. I remember, several years ago, when I was trying to read my Bible through from beginning to end, I dreaded coming to Deuteronomy! Now God was teaching me, verse by verse, through those very pages. Dear friend, there is no part of Scripture that God cannot use to reveal Himself to us. "All Scripture is God-breathed and is useful for teaching, rebuking, correcting and training in righteousness, so that the man of God may be thoroughly equipped for every good work" (2 Timothy 3:16, 17).

I opened my Bible to Deuteronomy and began to read in chapter 29, a chapter about the covenants God had made with His people. I remember asking, *Lord, what does this have to do with me?* I think that the Lord must have been smiling as He watched me, just waiting for my reaction as I kept reading.

Then I got to verse twelve. "You are standing here in order to enter into a covenant with the LORD your God, a covenant the LORD is making with you this day and sealing with an oath, to confirm you this day as his people, that he may be your God as he promised you and as he swore to your fathers, Abraham, Isaac and Jacob" (Deuteronomy 29:12, 13).

My heart began to race as I read those words. I felt like God was talking right to me. I felt that God was telling me that He wanted to make a covenant with me! *How is that possible?* I wondered. *Why would You want to make a covenant with me?* Surely I had not understood these verses correctly. This was God talking to the Israelites of old, wasn't it?

I reread those words and continued on to the following verses. "I am making this covenant, with its oath, not only with you who are standing here with us today in the presence of the LORD our God but also with those who are not here today" (Deuteronomy 29:14, 15).

Oh Father! I cried as my hand began to shake and my eyes filled, *Lord, is this for real?* I was stunned. What did this mean? The last words of that verse surely did include me! I knew in my heart that this was one of those moments that become a turning point, a pivotal experience; that from this point on, things would never be the same. Was I ready to accept that kind of change? What would be involved?

We are told in Hebrews 4:12 that Scripture is living and active. God can and does use words written centuries ago to reach down into our hearts and touch them with His love. He does guide and teach us through Scripture! And for me, this was one of those times.

My initial reaction was one of wonder and awe. How humbling to think that the Master of the universe wanted to establish a covenant with me! After the initial astonishment began to fade, the doubt and fear crept in. Surely, I'd misunderstood! Yet in my heart of hearts, I knew the invitation was real. And I was terribly frightened!

I began to back away mentally, emotionally, and spiritually, frightened by what I imagined a commitment like this might involve. After all, I reasoned, God has asked His children to do some pretty bizarre things! For the next day and a half, I put my fears and thoughts regarding this revelation on the back burners of my mind. I played in the lake, lounged on the beach, and read a good book. But the "call to covenant" was never far from my thoughts. I knew I needed to respond, to give God an answer. It's certainly a good thing that He is so patient with His children!

By the next day, I knew that, whatever this covenant involved, I was willing to enter into it. When I told Sylvia about my decision and expressed my confusion as to what kind of covenant God would want to make with me, she said, "Pat, I know exactly what kind of covenant this is, but it is something that you will have to discover on your own." I was somewhat puzzled by her certainty, but resolved to find the answer.

When we returned from our week at the lake, I still was not sure that I was reading God's message right in this instance, but I was willing to find out. I figured that if this call to covenant was for real, God would continue to lead me in that direction.

My first step was to look up the words *promise* and *covenant* in my dictionary.

Covenant is rather an archaic term. In today's language, we'd use the word *contract* or *agreement* or perhaps *pledge*. A covenant is a promise. Notice the similar definitions:

> *Promise*: (1) A declaration that one will do or refrain from doing something specified. (2) A legally binding declaration that gives the person to whom it is made a

right to expect or to claim the performance or forbearance of specified act.

Covenant: (1) Usually a formal, solemn, and binding agreement. (2) A written agreement or promise under seal between two or more parties especially for the performance of some action.

Both are promises, both can be considered legally binding. However, a covenant is often written or sealed as a sign of intent. So often we make promises we intend to keep, but frequently we forget them as soon as they are made. However, if we sign a contract, we are much less likely to forget the terms of the agreement! A covenant is not to be undertaken lightly.

Next, I took out my Bible concordance and began a systematic search for the word *covenant* in the Scriptures. I looked up each text, reading it in context and summarizing the information relating to the covenant. It was fascinating! Who instigated the covenant process? What kind of agreement was it? What were the terms? Was there a sign of the agreement? Was there a time length involved? Does a covenant have to be agreed to by both parties? As I found the answers to these questions, I learned more about the covenants recorded in Scripture, but I still didn't know what kind of covenant God would possibly want with me. I continued to pray that God would teach me to love Him with all my heart and that He would show me what He wanted. Sometimes God has to use someone else to get His message through to us. In my case, he used a stranger.

I had seen announcements for meetings being held in our local church, but I thought they were only for those who were members of a group called Light Bearers.* One of the speakers listed was Ty Gibson. I knew he was an author and thought it might be interesting to hear him speak but assumed the meetings were not open to the public. I was wrong.

I was getting my hair cut when, out of the blue, my hairdresser asked if I was going to attend any of the meetings! She was so excited about them and told me all were welcome. The 3:00 P.M. meeting was only a couple hours away, but right then I made plans to attend. Ty Gibson was giving a workshop, How to Study the Bible for Rapid Spiritual Growth. Catchy title, huh! I was very curious to see what he might have to say. It turned out to be a rendezvous planned by God.

That very first workshop, Ty referred to the Scriptures as being a love letter from God to show us His heart and that they were given to us so that we can develop a love relationship with Him and get to know Him intimately. As I listened to Ty's presentation, it was as if God were saying, "Pat, there is nothing better I would like to do for you than to reveal anew my love. Please come into My presence, get to know who I am. I want to talk with you." I was blown away! It was as if God had orchestrated this whole series of events. And I couldn't wait to hear more.

I purchased a copy of Ty Gibson's book *An Endless Falling in Love* and began to read it as soon as I got home. Ty spoke each morning, and as I listened to his sermons, I started to see God in a whole new light. It was as if I were being introduced to Someone that I had never met. Scripture portrayed a God such as I had never before seen. Such love! Such passion! Such an amazing capacity for love! A God who risked the very fabric of heaven itself to win my heart! As I continued to read and study, I began to understand that God wanted to make a covenant of that kind of love with me! The very thought brought me to my knees. Oh how I had misunderstood who He was!

Friend, Satan does not want you to see God as He is. He wants you to believe and accept some distorted image. Do you remember how worried I was that God would ask me to do something I wouldn't want to do, that He would require of me more than I wanted to give? What a warped image of God those thoughts reveal! His love for me is deeper than my mind and heart can begin to imagine. I know how much I love my children, yet God's love for me surpasses that love! Would He ask anything that would bring sorrow or pain? Would I ask that of my children? Jesus tried to tell us that in His Sermon on the Mount. " 'Which of you, if his son asks for bread, will give him a stone? Or if he asks for a fish, will give him a snake? If you, then, though you are evil, know how to give good gifts to your children, how much more will your Father in heaven give good gifts to those who ask him!' " (Matthew 7:9–11). How is it possible that I had never seen this before? God's love motivates everything He does. There is no motivation for Him other than love!

That week of meetings ended with a truly amazing climax. As Ty's last presentation drew to a close, he proposed that we enter into a Covenant of Love with our Maker and Redeemer, the God who longs to have an intimate friendship with each one of us. He began handing out pieces of paper printed with this Covenant of Love that we could keep as a reminder of our contract with the Almighty. As you can expect, when he began to talk about signing a covenant, I began to cry. I am sure that those around me wondered what was wrong. They had no idea what impact Ty's simple invitation had on my heart. God had answered my questions. He supplied the missing pieces. I am sure He laughed out loud with joy as I signed my name on that piece of paper. I keep it in my Bible, and whenever I am tempted to think that God is too busy to hear my prayers, when I am discouraged and disheartened, I can take out that piece of paper and remember that God loves me with His whole being; there is nothing He would not do for my ultimate happiness. He wants us to see Him as He is.

Was this series of events just coincidence? It's possible, I suppose, but I don't think so. I believe God provided an opportunity that opened my eyes, enabled me to see, and showed me how I could love Him with the kind of love I was praying for. For me, love was the only possible response when I came to know and see Him as He truly is. And it began with a yearning to learn about love.

In the coming chapter, Sylvia will tell you how this part of my journey affected hers. God loves helping us so that we can help those around us! And as I talked with Sylvia about what I was learning, it ignited in her a longing to learn more. Stay tuned!

಄಄

Father God,

You are a covenant-making and covenant-keeping God. Forgive my mistrust and teach me anew that You are a God motivated only by Your great love for Your children. Help me to let go of my fears and to embrace the plans You have for my life. Amen.

---

*Light Bearers is a nonprofit ministry whose purpose is to help proclaim the gospel of the Lord Jesus Christ through the spoken and the published word. (Light Bearers Ministry can be contacted at www.lbm.org.)

*Never be lacking in zeal, but keep your spiritual
fervor, serving the Lord.*
—Romans 12:11

*It is not good to have zeal without knowledge,
nor to be hasty and miss the way.*
—Proverbs 19:2

Chapter 9

Passion

Passion.

What colors would you use to paint a picture of passion? Inky darks, icy pastels, or quiet neutrals? Hmm . . . I don't think so! Passion calls for brilliant colors, intense hues with fiery depths, and dramatic contrasts! Passion demands movement and excitement! A portrait of passion draws you in, creating a desire within your heart to experience its power.

Passion!

Let's focus on mental, emotional, and spiritual passion— and not on physical passion, which the word might first bring to mind. How might we explain emotional or spiritual passion? Zeal? Enthusiasm? Intense desire? Compulsion?

One definition of *passion* is "an intense, driving, overmastering feeling or conviction."

Originally the word came from the Greek word *passus* or *passio,* meaning "suffering or agony," as of a martyr. That's why the suffering of Christ on the cross is often referred to as "the Passion" and plays depicting that event are called "Passion plays."

Larry Lichtenwalter defines *passion* as "being compelled to action."[1] He says it is a force within people that drives them far beyond ordinary activities. Being passionate about something means being excited enough that you will actually *do* something about it.

Wow! Have you ever known someone who was passionate? Have you ever experienced that kind of passion yourself? What in your life creates that kind of deep emotion? For some, passion is a way of life; they greet each day with a zest for living! What is your passion? Some would say they are passionate about their kids; I would say I am passionate about my work. Some would respond they are passionate about scrapbooking or cooking or crafts or sports. What compels you to action? What lights the fire within you?

Erwin McManus says he wonders how many of us are passionate about anything.[2] For many of us, passion seems to require too much effort, too much time, and we feel our stores of both are sorely depleted. We are more comfortable just drifting along. We are too tired or too busy to contemplate becoming passionate about anything.

Do you remember the steps of my journey outlined earlier in this book?

1. I need You to help me.
2. Help me to know You.
3. Help me to love You.
4. Help me to be passionate about You.

We have arrived at step four. Passion. Another intangible. Another emotion I have no ability to create within myself. Yet one of the things I've discovered is that God desires passion.

As I began thinking about the areas of passion in my life,

I realized again that my passion is my business. *Is that a bad thing?* I wondered. Are there good passions and bad passions? Surely the Scriptures would provide an answer, so with a prayer for enlightenment, I began another journey in the Scriptures.

My first stop was the story of Phinehas, found in Numbers 25. I had never heard of Phinehas, but in this story, he kills an Israelite man and a Midianite woman for flagrantly and openly defying God. He was defending God's honor.

> The LORD said to Moses, "Phinehas son of Eleazar, the son of Aaron, the priest, has turned my anger away from the Israelites; for he was as zealous as I am for my honor among them, so that in my zeal I did not put an end to them. Therefore tell him I am making my covenant of peace with him. He and his descendants will have a covenant of a lasting priesthood, because he was zealous for the honor of his God and made atonement for the Israelites" (Numbers 25:10–13).

What in the world is God trying to tell me? I asked myself. *Does passion for God result in fanaticism?* That possibility concerned me.

I was next led to the story of Paul, who persecuted and killed the early Christians, zealously defending God's honor. So, what was the difference? My questions grew. Then God led me to study about David and Goliath.

David slew the giant Goliath, not because he wanted to show off his muscle, boost his ego, or prove his manhood but because Goliath was a Philistine defaming David's Friend and Companion, his God. God was very real and personal to David.

Hmm . . . wasn't that what Phinehas was doing too? Defending God's honor? Then what about Paul? Didn't he believe he was persecuting people for God's honor, although God eventually showed him otherwise?

Then I began to see verses like these: "It is fine to be zealous, provided the purpose is good, and to be so always" (Galatians 4:18). "Whatever you do, work at it with all your heart, as working for the Lord, not for men, since you know that you will receive an inheritance from the Lord as a reward. It is the Lord Christ you are serving" (Colossians 3:23, 24). "Whether you eat or drink or whatever you do, do it all for the glory of God" (1 Corinthians 10:31).

Those passages led to the question, How am I to tell the difference between what is an acceptable object of passion and what isn't? I was drawn again to the story of David.

I am learning so much from his life! God called David a man after His own heart. What was it about David that struck a responsive chord in the heart of the Father? It was his passion!

Ty Gibson helps us understand: "In David God saw a heart like His own, a heart with which He could resonate and beat in unison. This shepherd boy who became king was a man of great strength who was in touch with the emotional side of his nature. He was a courageous king *and* a passionate poet. The most emotionally sensitive approaches to God in Scripture were penned by David's hand and sung by his lips."[3]

Philip Yancey puts it this way: "I keep thumbing back to the story of David because I know no better model for a passionate relationship with God than the king named David. His very name meant 'beloved.'. . . As a man of passion, David felt more passionately about God than about anything else in the world, and during his reign that message trickled down to the entire nation."[4]

David's very life was filled with his passion for God! "David opened his heart to God, loved God, believed God, thought about God, imagined God, addressed God, prayed to God, sang to God, obeyed God—in other words, framed his whole world with God."[5] And although he "blew it" often and regularly, his passion for God carried him through. I ache to have a passion for God like that!

Maybe that's the key. David was passionate about God and anything that God was passionate about! He used his God as a measuring stick. And God's motivation is always love.

Shortly after my return home from the lake house, I was telling Gail about all that had transpired there. Her excitement grew as I shared the message I felt God wanted me to share with the women at the upcoming retreat.

"Oh, Sylvia! You just have to read the new book by Ty Gibson I was telling you about!" Gail loves to read as much as Pat does, and between the two of them, I always have a lengthy "must read" list.

"I will pick up a copy for you and bring it to our lunch meeting next week!"

I could tell she was very enthusiastic, and I admit the title, *An Endless Falling in Love*, piqued my interest. I didn't know it at the time, but the next step in my journey had begun.

Several days later, I got another phone call, this time from Pat. As she shared all that was happening in her life, what she was learning about covenants, and what was being revealed in the meetings she was attending, her enthusiasm was contagious. And she told me I just had to read Ty Gibson's newest book, *An Endless Falling in Love*.

There it was again! That same book! I had two friends, in two different places, pointing me in the same direction. Coincidence? I don't think so. I think God was gently prodding, leading me on to the next step.

It was a week or so later when I finally picked up my copy of this book that had such impact on the lives of my friends. I was eager to see whether it would affect my relationship with God or sharpen my picture of Him.

Opening to the first page, I read,

"As I passed by again,
I saw that the time had come
For you to fall in love.
I covered your naked body with My coat
And promised to love you.
Yes, I made a marriage covenant with you,
And you became Mine."
This is what the Sovereign Lord says.
Ezekiel 16:8, TEV

My initial reaction was shock! I had never before read anything like this in the Bible. I got out my Bible and began to read from the beginning of Ezekiel 16.

This is really gross! I thought to myself. The passage relates the bloody birth of an unwanted child who was despised and cast aside. But I kept on reading. As I got to verse eight again, I felt my heart drawn in. The words reached out and grabbed my imagination.

How does this passage relate to me? I wondered.

As I continued to study and as I remembered all that Pat had shared with me, I began to see what she had seen. My heart broke and I wept. Once again, God had both of us on the same spiritual path. He knew just how thickheaded I can be, and He knew I would need some help to understand this. So, once again, He used my friend Pat. As she explained what she was learning and what God was revealing about Himself to her, I began to see and understand too!

God is the One who rescued me! God is the One who cleaned me up! God was passing by again and, seeing me, knew that the time was right for me to fall in love! To fall in love with Him! God covered my nakedness, my sinfulness, with His coat and promised to love me! And I became His.

I wept then because I remembered God's promise to me that we were going to have an amazing relationship as a result of my willingness to accept this invitation to speak. I actually felt His love so much that it is difficult for me to describe it.

And this was just the first page of the book. Imagine what else was in store for me!

Each day I read one chapter and studied the Bible texts used. I was absolutely amazed at the picture of God that was shining through the Scriptures I read! Here is a God of passion! I was humbled to learn how deep is His love and passion for me! It was a new and wondrous facet of His character that I had only glimpsed before, and as He revealed more to my heart and mind, I got more and more excited!

God has been so misunderstood down through the ages by so many of His children. He is not the stern taskmaster we so often perceive, ready to punish all who step out of line. That's a lie Satan would have us believe. In truth, God loves you more than He loves His own well-being. Heaven was forever changed when Christ came to dwell among men and women.

The triune fellowship the Godhead enjoyed in ages past was permanently altered. And Christ risked everything to redeem you and me! That kind of passion and love is hard for us to accept and understand. In our self-centered natures, a love that is always other-centered seems so foreign and too good to be true.[6]

Ty Gibson coined a new word to describe God's passion—omnipassionate.[7] God is omnipotent: all powerful, omniscient: all knowing, omnipresent: all present, and as the Creator of emotion and feeling, He is also omnipassionate: all passionate. And, friend, He is passionate about you! His descent into your world and into your life, and His sacrifice for you on Calvary's cross, demonstrate beyond question and understanding His passionate desire to claim you as His own. But the choice to refuse or accept remains yours.

What I discovered as I continued to study is that like love, passion is a response. When you finally begin to accept and believe the truth about God's character, when you realize the depth of His love for you, love is awakened! Likewise, once His passion for you is perceived, passion is aroused! How can you not get excited about a God like this?

Here is a God of deep and flaming passion. . . .

. . . He agonizes over the fact that we are oblivious to that incredible love. . . . [Jesus] has "declared" the beauty of God's character to our darkened eyes and deaf ears. And this He has done with a solitary purpose in mind: to draw us into the intimate circle of love that flows and surges between Himself and the Father. He yearns with deep desire that we, yes, you and me, would forever live in the pleasurable current of God's glorious love.[8]

I found myself face to face with a God of passion! If I were to respond in kind, passion to passion, what would that involve? What are the characteristics of passion? Larry Lichtenwalter explains it this way:

1. Passion *claims it all.*
2. Passion *yields it all.*
3. Passion is *imaginative.*
4. Passion *constantly renews itself.*
5. Passion *hears what it wants to hear.*
6. Passion *has purpose, a reason for being, an agenda.*
7. Passion *haunts the imagination.*
8. Passion *evokes passion.*[9]

Are you feeling a bit overwhelmed? When I consider the love and passion God has demonstrated to me and for me, I hardly know how to respond! Can this be real? Is it true? Ah, dear friend, God longs for us to respond to His love! He is passionate about entering into an intimate relationship with us! Larry Lichtenwalter gives us additional insight:

"Each one of these facets of passion revolves around one inescapable reality—passion is deeply personal. It is experienced and expressed by a personal being—you, me, or God. . . .

"Because passion deals largely with the heart, it involves the meaning of our lives and the purpose of our existence. It expresses who we are deep inside—our values, our choices, our sense of reality, our creativity, what captures our imagination, what we're willing to commit ourselves to, and what we truly love."[10]

Does God want a people of passion? He certainly does!

Are you ready for a trip into passion? Be prepared. It's a five-ticket ride like no other!

☙❧

Dear passionate Father,

Create in us a passionate heart. Consume us with Your over-whelming love. Draw us into the intimate circle of that love, developing in us a passionate response. Amen.

---

1. Larry Lichtenwalter, *David: A Heart Like His* (Hagerstown, Md.: Review and Herald® Publishing Association, 2003), 13.

2. Erwin McManus, *Uprising: A Revolution of the Soul* (Nashville, Tenn.: Nelson Books, 2003), 13.

3. Ty Gibson, *An Endless Falling in Love* (Nampa, Idaho: Pacific Press® Publishing Association, 2003), 105.

4. Philip Yancey, *Reaching for the Invisible God* (Grand Rapids, Mich.: Zondervan Publishing House, 2000), 190.

5. Lichtenwalter, *David,* 127.

6. Gibson, *Endless Falling in Love,* 14.

7. Ibid., chapter 12, 99–107.

8. Ibid., 7, 8.

9. Lichtenwalter, *David,* 125, 126.

10. Ibid., 126.

The Lord your God is testing you to find out whether you love him with all your heart and with all your soul. It is the Lord your God you must follow, and him you must revere. Keep his commands and obey him, serve him and hold fast to him.
—*Deuteronomy 13:3, 4*

Chapter 10

Hold Fast

The letdown. It always comes. It follows every exciting event in our lives, every major happening we anticipate with joy, be it a vacation, a visit from family or friends far away, a major move, or a new job. We bustle about making plans and preparations, eagerly looking forward to the moments ahead. Then, suddenly, it's over, and the letdown sets in.

As vice president of finance at Ripley's Believe It or Not! part of my job was to visit all the museums and conduct surprise audits. (Well, somebody's got to do it!) Our museum in Australia was next on the list, and I was looking forward to this opportunity to visit the land down under. Because I knew I would be working long hours, I decided that some vacation time was in order and planned a week's vacation following a week of work. And to my delight, my husband thought two weeks of vacation in Australia sounded wonderful, so he arranged time off to come with me.

For weeks we pored over travel guides and brochures, planning carefully each day of our trip. We wanted to squeeze as

107

much as possible into the seven days of free time I would have. Finally the day of departure arrived!

What a grueling trip! After thirty hours of travel, we arrived in Sydney, weary but excited. We arrived on a weekend, and it was hot! January in Australia is midsummer! We planned to tour Sydney for a day before heading to Brisbane. We just couldn't go to Sydney without seeing the famed Sydney Opera House and taking the Sydney Harbor cruise. Then we headed for the Blue Mountains and spectacular scenery!

Then we were off to Brisbane and on to the Gold Coast—back to the "attractions" world. Each day my husband, Warren, would walk me to work while heading to the beach. I was a bit jealous because he was getting a great tan while I was stuck inside reviewing numbers!

Only five days more, I kept reminding myself, *then we will be off to Cairns! Beautiful rainforests and the Great Barrier Reef!* Then it was, *Only four more days . . .* I could hardly wait.

At last the day arrived when we were to catch our flight to Cairns. Warren was wearing a golf shirt with the Maroons rugby team logo on it. When the check-in clerk saw it, she wondered if Warren was a part of the national rugby team it commemorated. Clearly he was not, our Canadian accents giving us away, but she was very kind and upgraded our seats to first class! What a wonderful start to my week of vacation!

For the next week, we enjoyed forays into the rainforest, hugging koala bears, and walking among kangaroos. Each day was a new adventure. We had seen pictures of the Great Barrier Reef, but nothing prepared us for the beauty we encountered on our catamaran tour. Tropical fish I'd never seen or imagined and blue, blue water with coral brilliant in the sunshine. So much beauty, always changing! I didn't want to miss anything. I wanted to stay out there forever!

Day after day we explored the area, and still there remained so much to see. As the time to leave drew near, I tried to postpone our flight home, but no seats were available. It was time to go home and resume everyday life. The thought of returning to work, to the world of mail and laundry and bills, was depressing. The letdown set in.

Have you been there? Can you relate? How I hate that feeling! And yet it's a seemingly inevitable reaction. After the mountaintop comes the valley. It's true not only with the events of our days but in our spiritual walk as well.

After the spiritual high I experienced at the lake house, you would think that my excitement and passion would continue to grow and that each day would be greeted as a new adventure in knowing God. But that's not what happened. I began what I call a downward slide. There were days when I could not sense God's presence, days when I did not feel His love, days when I questioned whether everything I had learned or experienced was real.

"How can that be?" you may ask.

Reality sets in. For each of us, life is a struggle. We want to remain in that wonderful state of spiritual awareness, we want to remain on a spiritual high, but suddenly we are confronted by our everyday tasks and responsibilities. Time becomes a precious commodity, and we must choose how we use the minutes in our day. Satan is delighted to offer a myriad of opportunities to distract us. He uses the tools of doubt and guilt to turn our hearts away from the only One who can help us.

Paul talks about just this situation in his letter to the Romans. "I do not understand what I do. . . . For I have the desire to do what is good, but I cannot carry it out. For what I do is not the good I want to do; no, the evil I do not want to do—this I keep on doing" (Romans 7:15–19).

Isn't it nice to know that someone like Paul went through the same frustrations you and I face?

As Pat and I were preparing to leave our retreat at the lake house, we came across a remedy for this situation that I'd like to share with you. Perhaps it will help you the next time you find yourself in a spiritual slide.

Well, when you feel you've lost your spiritual edge or passion, the secret to restoration is embodied in two words: Hold fast! Those two little words yield so much power once you begin to understand what's involved.

Shortly after our time at the lake house, when I began my downward slide, Pat was still on a spiritual climb. But I knew that sooner or later, she, too, would experience a letdown.

Before we left the lake, we made a pact. We promised each other that we would be there through thick and thin and that we would always remind each other to hold fast.

As we had talked and studied that week, those two little words seemed to pop up everywhere. Several verses in Deuteronomy come to mind.

- Moses urged the children of Israel to "love the Lord your God, to walk in all his ways and to hold fast to him" (Deuteronomy 11:22).
- "The Lord your God is testing you to find out whether you love him with all your heart and with all your soul. It is the Lord your God you must follow, and him you must revere. Keep his commands and obey him; serve him and hold fast to him" (Deuteronomy 13:3, 4).

- "Love the LORD your God, listen to his voice, and hold fast to him. For the LORD is your life" (Deuteronomy 30:20).

"Perhaps God is trying to tell us something here," Pat said one afternoon. "I think that these two words are going to become a watch-word between the two of us!"

God wants us to love Him with all our hearts and souls and minds and strength, and He wants us to hang onto Him for all we are worth! Hold fast! When you feel yourself begin to question and doubt, hold fast! When you get discouraged and disheartened, hold fast, dear friend!

I am convinced that the Holy Spirit made these two words stand out to us, because He knew the trials and temptations that were coming, and He wanted us to have the means to cope.

Well, sure enough, it wasn't long before "hurricane Sylvia" began to brew. When I go out of town or get outside of my normal routine, finding or making time for quiet devotions and solitude is a real struggle. The lake house experience took place in June, and in July, my husband and I went on our annual vacation to Canada.

You would think that vacation would afford time to wind down, time to reflect and indulge in those quiet moments of solitude, but that's not what happens with me. We were with friends, and the kids were up, ready to go, early every morning. The cabin was brewing with activity, and quiet itself became illusive. I knew I was going to have to get creative.

So I took longer in the bathroom and went off by myself for walks. I had brought along several books to read, and I took them with me to the pool. And although it wasn't ideal, I knew that I had to hold fast. Evenings were somewhat better. I could go to bed a little earlier than the rest and read. I read

Ty Gibson's book *An Endless Falling in Love*; then I'd pray before falling asleep. I learned that I had to choose to make the time.

A few weeks later I traveled to England on business, and I really struggled with this issue. There were days when there was just no time for study or prayer! I discovered that I really missed having some quiet time with my Lord. I found myself yearning for time in His presence. My days just didn't seem right without that daily contact.

And then I got into some really dodgy territory. I missed more than one day, and the more days I missed, the easier it became to make excuses. The hunger for time with Jesus began to subside. When I realized what was happening, it frightened me. I prayed, asking God to help me find the necessary moments. "Lord, please awaken me early in the morning, so that I will have an uninterrupted hour to spend with You."

And you know something? He did! Now, I am not a morning person, but I was wide awake and couldn't have gone back to sleep if I had tried! I spent a good forty-five minutes with Him that morning before I had to get ready for a meeting.

"Wow!" I thought. "How easy it is to get used to starting the day without Him, but how much better to keep that appointment!" I remembered those two little words, *hold fast!* They seemed to take on new meaning in my heart. God wants us to hold fast to Him, and if we ask, He will supply the power and strength to do just that!

A few years ago, a friend told me that she had to drive to downtown Nashville for her job and had to be there by eight o'clock in the morning. Because the drive time was about an hour, she had to leave her home shortly after seven, which meant that in order to have a few quiet moments with her Lord, she got up at five o'clock in the morning! That blew my mind. That conversation has stayed with me because I saw a Christian woman who was "seeking first His kingdom"—even if it meant getting up at five o'clock.

My sister-in-law, who has two small children, will get up at five o'clock so that she has a quiet hour with her Lord before the younger of the two wakes up at six-thirty. These two women are holding fast, and their relationship with Jesus shows it. Yes, there is an obedience factor in all of this, but the obedience comes from their love for their Lord and Creator.

What about me? My obedience comes from knowing that my day just isn't right if I start it without Him. This time is a gift He has given me, and when I miss that appointment, I also miss the gift He's waiting to bestow. I miss Him when I choose to ignore the appointment.

Another thing that helps me to hold fast is having an accountability partner. When I was in England, I received an e-mail every couple days from Pat, reminding me to hold fast! So, find yourself an accountability partner, one who will encourage you, one who will keep reminding you of how much God loves you and is longing for an intimate friendship with you, one who will remind you to hold fast! And if that's not possible, write yourself a few notes and put them up where you will see them, and each time you see that note, ask God to help you. He will! Maintaining your passion for Jesus is worth whatever effort it takes, dear friend!

We hold fast by the same means that brought the knowledge of God's love to our hearts in the first place. Ty Gibson puts it this way: "As we become born again by the realization of God's love at the foot of the cross, so we are to maintain our new life by remaining under the powerful influence of the cross."[1]

Gibson continues: "The concept is simple: The more distant from our thoughts is the cross of Christ, the stronger will be the appeals of temptation. The greater is our conscious appreciation of the cross, the mightier will be the heart's will to vanquish sin."[2]

We need to spend time "beholding" our Lord. We need to keep our eyes focused on Him. "Beholding is the deliberate action of the mind to focus, meditate, or dwell upon a matter in order to gain a clear understanding of it."[3] It is at the cross that His passionate love played itself out for the universe to see. How easy it is for us to forget, to become distracted, pulled in different directions by our families, our jobs, our desires.

The author of a beautiful account of Christ's life says, "It would be well for us to spend a thoughtful hour each day in contemplation of the life of Christ."[4] That's beholding, friend!

> Through the cross of Christ God demonstrated His matchless love toward us in order to move and empower us to cease living for ourselves and to live for His glory in conscious response to His love. . . .
> . . . The Lord intends that His love be far more to us than an emotionally stimulating idea. He wants it to be an experiential reality for us, to touch every aspect of our lives with healing, overcoming power.[5]

And God does not leave you alone, dear friend, struggling to hang on. No matter where you are, He will find you.

> Where can I go from your Spirit?
> Where can I flee from your presence?

If I go up to the heavens, you are there;
    if I make my bed in the depths, you are there.
If I rise on the wings of the dawn,
    if I settle on the far side of the sea,
even there your hand will guide me,
    your right hand will hold me fast (Psalm 139:7–10).

The power of love.
    The power of passion.
        The power of the cross.
            Hold fast!

❦

Loving Creator,

Thank You for risking the universe to save us by choosing death on a cross. Help us to understand the magnitude of that supreme act so we can hold fast in those times we are tempted to give up. Thank You for holding us even "faster" with Your loving hand and never losing Your grip. Never let us go! Amen.

1. Ty Gibson, *In the Light of God's Love* (Nampa, Idaho: Pacific Press® Publishing Association, 1996), 66.

2. Ibid., 67.

3. Ibid., 123.

4. Ellen G. White, *The Desire of Ages* (Nampa, Idaho: Pacific Press® Publishing Association, 1940), 83.

5. Gibson, *Light*, 121.

*We know that in all things God works for the good
of those who love him, who have been called
according to his purpose.*
—Romans 8:28

Chapter 11

Lemonade

What do you think of when you hear the word *lemon*? A sunny yellow fruit? A fresh clean smell? A mouth-puckering tartness? The car that's given you nothing but headaches? Lemons. Sometimes, it seems that our lives are full of lemons. Sometimes we think of ourselves as lemons—soured by life, of little use to God or anyone else. So what's a person to do?

Ah, dear friend, that's the time to remember the One who created the lemon tree. He has a purpose for each piece of fruit. Each lemon has value. Just look at what can be done with a lemon! On a hot, humid summer day, what tastes better than a tall, cool glass of lemonade? That tartness makes a thirst-quenching delight! Lemon meringue pie is always a winner on a dessert menu. The lemon is used to clean, to flavor, to preserve, to scent, and to relieve ailments. If human beings have found so many uses for this small, sour, acidic fruit, imagine what the Creator can accomplish!

Our journey together began with the four steps I discovered as I sought answers to my questions about God.

1. I need You to help me.
2. Help me to know You.
3. Help me to love You.
4. Help me to be passionate about You.

It was only when I was broken that I realized I needed to look up. It was only then that I asked for help. I then had to let go of some things in my life that I had considered important.

We've explored several ways we can get to know this God of love, ways we can experience His very real presence in our lives: Bible study, prayer, silence, and solitude in developing an intimate relationship with Him.

We've talked together about our need for heart circumcision that only God can perform. He alone is the Divine Surgeon creating in us the desire and ability to love Him with all that we are and have. That procedure at times can be painful, but the resulting changes are liberating! He then can fill our hearts with love and passion.

We've learned that God is anxious to help us maintain an intimate friendship with Him, and He will do all in His power to hold fast to us!

Are you beginning to sense that there is nothing God will not do to reach you? Has that truth impressed itself in your thoughts? No lemon in your life is too difficult, too rotten to be salvaged by your Creator. He can make something beautiful out of the refuse! We need to let go, to loosen our grip on that refuse. We need to turn control over to Him. This was a lesson that God was still trying to teach me.

I was enthusiastic about the lessons I had learned as I prepared for talks I was to give at the Kentucky-Tennessee Women's Retreat. God was leading me step by step, but it just wasn't quite coming together. I was still scared. Would this be something that women of all walks of life would find helpful? Could I present it in an engaging manner? What could I do to help make a lasting impact on the lives of those women? Then I got a phone call from the Women's Ministries leader of the Carolina Conference. She asked me if I would speak the last weekend of September at a weekend women's retreat they were having in Wilmington, North Carolina.

My first thought was *No way! I have to prepare for the Kentucky-Tennessee Women's Retreat. I can't possibly do both!* When I told the Women's Ministries director my concerns about the timing, she was very encouraging and suggested I use the same material and do a "dry run." I had to chuckle at the suggestion and thought, *OK, Lord, if this is what You want me to do, I'll do it!*

I was not sure just what God wanted me to say, but I agreed to go. About two weeks before that event, I was still at a loss as to what God wanted me to present. I was praying intently one morning during my quiet time, when I was impressed to listen to one of Ty Gibson's sermons that I had on CD. I resisted, not seeing any connection. The impression persisted. God works that way sometimes, doesn't He? As I listened to that sermon CD, the message came across loud and clear!

Ty Gibson's sermon was based on Isaiah 40:9:

You who bring good tidings to Zion,
    go up on a high mountain.
You who bring good tidings to Jerusalem,
    lift up your voice with a shout,
lift it up, do not be afraid;

say to the towns of Judah,
"Here is your God!"

There it was. The message God wanted to share through me, through my story. His character has been so misconstrued through the ages, His motives and actions misrepresented and misunderstood. What He wanted me to share was the Being I discovered, a God of forgiveness and compassion, of infinite patience, a God of incomparable love, a God of passion! "Here is your God!"

"That's it!" I squealed. "You want me to help correct all those misconceptions I had about You and to declare the truth about You to the women of the Carolina Conference." I got very excited about the possibility.

And it was a wonderful opportunity to try out some of the material I'd prepared. My topic would work in nicely with the theme of the weekend—beholding God. One of the exercises I planned to use at the Kentucky-Tennessee retreat to close the meetings was to have each woman make a glass of lemonade using a recipe I'd prepared. Each ingredient represented some facet of God's work in our lives, and I was sure that this exercise would provide the impact I wanted to achieve. So with that in mind, I decided to give this exercise a trial run in Wilmington.

It was a good thing I did. The activity turned out to be almost a disaster! Each woman was given a glass, water, lemons, sugar, and a stirring stick. What a mess as each tried to squeeze the lemons, add the ingredients, and stir them together. The room was filled with laughter and talking. Water sloshed out of the glasses, spilling the sugared liquid and generally making a mess. If this didn't work with fifty women, it would be a monumental disaster with two hundred fifty! While I was relieved to discover this before using the activity in Tennessee, I was left with no closing exercise. I panicked! It was back to the drawing board and back down on my knees. I had only one week to come up with something else.

God already had an answer to my dilemma. I just needed to listen. Funny, isn't it, how we worry and fuss when what we most need to do is pray and listen? Instead of having each woman make a glass of lemonade, I invited several of the attendees to share an experience during which God had taken the lemons they were experiencing and made lemonade from them. As the women shared their experiences, they cut the lemons, squeezed out the juice, added water and sugar, and stirred it all together. When they had finished, we talked about the process and the ingredients: the pain sometimes involved when God's scalpel circumcises our hearts, the squeezing that occurs as we surrender our lives and become an empty vessel for Him to fill, the cleansing that takes place as our lives are washed clean in the pure water that is His alone, the sweetness of the Holy Spirit as He takes up residence in our hearts, and the stirring of our souls as we realize what He has done for us. Lemonade!

I was humbled as the audience responded to the women as they shared their stories. Many were touched as they related to those experiences. It was a much more meaningful exercise than any I could have come up with, and God knew just what was needed and what would work. As a result, not only did those attending come away with a memorable experience, God again taught this daughter a lesson about His provisions.

Lemonade!

The experience of speaking at this event taught me again how God can make lemonade of our trials and troubles. It may have been my topic, but God was still revealing Himself to me in unusual ways. The second weekend of this retreat was for me more difficult. It was the weekend that many friends from my church family were planning to attend. What would they think of me? It added to the nervousness I felt as the time came to address another two hundred fifty women. The responsibility seemed overwhelming. And to make matters worse, I developed an ear infection. I was feeling very vulnerable and inadequate.

Sabbath morning, Pat and I woke early and decided to go down to the lakeshore and spend a few moments praying and sharing. As we gathered together our things, I noticed my Bible was missing. I was sure I'd brought it down from the chapel, but I couldn't find it anywhere. Not wanting to waste more time looking, I grabbed my *Message* Bible and off we went. The sun was just coming over the hilltops. The lake was quiet. It was so peaceful. We both sat silently and gazed at the view.

After I breathed a prayer for guidance, that still, small Voice whispered to me to open my Bible to 2 Corinthians. *Hmm . . . I wonder what's in 2 Corinthians?*

> In the Messiah, in Christ, God leads us from place to place in one perpetual victory parade. Through us, he brings knowledge of Christ. Everywhere we go, people breathe in the exquisite fragrance. Because of Christ, we give off a sweet scent rising to God, which is recognized by those on the way of salvation—an aroma redolent with life. But those on the way to destruction treat us more like the stench from a rotting corpse.
>
> This is a terrific responsibility. Is anyone competent

to take it on? No—but at least we don't take God's Word, water it down, and then take it to the streets to sell it cheap. We stand in Christ's presence when we speak; God looks us in the face. We get what we say straight from God and say it as honestly as we can (2 Corinthians 2:14–17, *The Message*).

Tears streamed down my face. Once again, God heard the cry of my heart and gave me an answer. The words I read were just what I needed that morning, and had I taken my New International Version Bible, the words would not have been the same! *The Message* Bible was the one I needed, and my heavenly Father knew it. I was reassured that He would be with me as I stood in front of those women and that He would give me the right words to say. I would be standing in Christ's presence! God would look me in the face! That morning as I stood on the platform to speak, I noticed the sun shining through the stained-glass window at the rear of the chapel. It seemed to me that as I looked up, I could see the face of my Creator giving me the words these women needed to hear. I could feel His presence and His encouragement as I spoke. Does God take our fears and turn them into something wonderful? He certainly does!

Lemonade!

As the weekend drew to a close, many wonderful stories surfaced of the way God had touched those present, such as the woman who was walking in a park with her daughter and came across a retreat brochure lying on a park bench. She knew she needed something else in her life and thought perhaps she would find an answer there. Her daughter encouraged her to come even though she knew no one. As I talked about the steps of my journey, she was drawn by the similarities she saw in herself. Then there was the woman who frantically searched for me the last morning of the retreat to share a poem that had taken on new meaning for her as a result of her experiences there. After my return home, I received an e-mail from someone who had to hold fast the minute she got home and how the weekend had helped prepare her for the turmoil she faced.

Within days of my return home, I was surprised and delighted by the cards that came to my home. Never had I expected anything like that! One that really touched me was from the "Highland SDA Gals" who took the time to create and incorporate pictures of the weekend along with a Thank-you message: "We were truly blessed by your messages, and just wanted to tell you how much we appreciate you coming and sharing your story with all of us and encouraging us to let God make lemonade out of us lemons!"

I was overwhelmed by how God worked during those two weekends. I realized that it had nothing to do with me and all to do with Him.

"Sylvia, even though the message you gave each weekend was the same, the words you used were different," Pat commented as we were processing the two-weekend retreat.

I knew the Lord had changed some of the words I used because He knew each audience and I didn't. He knew just what each one present needed to hear and how the ideas needed to be expressed. He kept the promise He gave me in 2 Corinthians that Sabbath morning by the lake. He gave me the words He needed me to say. What an awesome experience!

As I come to the end of this part of my journey, I look back and am continually amazed at the way God was leading me from the minute I was born. Sometimes I was aware of it; most times I was not. But He is faithful. He has each of us on a very personal journey. Everyone has a story. Everyone was created for a purpose. Everyone was created to be lemonade!

Before I leave you to continue your journey, I'd like to give you one more example of how with God, all things are possible, and we must hold fast! He can make lemonade out of any situation if only we will let Him.

Do you remember in the earlier part of my journey, how my Catholic father was extremely concerned about the brainwashing he was sure his children would receive in that Saturday church? Remember the tension created in my home when my mom returned to her spiritual roots? That underlying tension remained until just a couple years ago. Oh, how my mother prayed for my father, day after day, year after year. We all prayed for him to see the Truth. We prayed that he would enter a personal relationship with his Creator.

Dad remained adamant in his opinions until shortly after his retirement. Every once in a while, when my mom was not feeling well, Dad offered to drive her to church. And he stayed to drive her home again. Though his visits were infrequent, he began to make some friends there. I could hardly believe that he was actually visiting church with my mom!

"Daddy, is Opa going to be in heaven?" my six-year-old niece, Courtney, asked my brother.

Raymond hardly knew how to respond. "I guess that will be up to Jesus," he replied.

"But, Daddy, Opa isn't a Christian like we are, is he?" she persisted.

"No, Opa isn't a Christian like we are—yet."

"What can we do?" she asked, concern written all over her little face.

"I think we need to pray about it," Raymond answered.

Six weeks later, my father began attending a local Adventist evangelistic series with my mom.

One morning, a few weeks later, he was visiting with my sister-in-law, Cathy. "I've been wrong all these years," he remarked. "No one but God has the power to change the Sabbath! I'm beginning to realize too that Jesus died for *me*, and I am thinking that I want to be a part of His family."

To say my sister-in-law was surprised would be a gross understatement. As soon as my dad left, she called me on the phone. "Sylvia, you are not going to believe what just happened!"

A few days later, my dad announced that he was going to be baptized.

I will never forget that Sabbath morning in the little church in Greenville, Tennessee, as our family watched my seventy-two-year-old dad walk down into the baptismal tank. He looked as peaceful as I've ever seen him look as he waited eagerly to "get dunked," as he had so often teased us.

Does God still answer prayer? Most certainly He does! We may become discouraged, we may feel that it's hopeless, but God just smiles, and when we least expect it, we discover that He still makes lemonade!

❧❧

Dear loving Father,

Thank You for always pursuing us. Thank You for loving us unconditionally and never giving up. Thank You for being the Master Lemonade Maker, using Your own personal recipe for each of us. How awesome is Your love! Open our eyes and help us to "connect the dots" so we can clearly see You working in our lives.

I pray that each reader of this book has been drawn closer to You as they read and that they have begun to truly "behold" You—the Awesome Creator, Redeemer, Savior, and Best Friend. Continue to circumcise our hearts and hold fast to us just as You have promised. Help us to hang on to You, becoming more passionate for You and only You. Amen.

Were you inspired by this book? You'll want to read the books Sylvia Matiko read by Ty Gibson, associate director/ speaker for Light Bearers Ministry.

In the Light of God's Love
Ty Gibson

Every now and then a book is written that penetrates beyond the head and speaks to the inmost heart. Page by page the reader senses the distinct moving of God's Spirit. Christ, in all His matchless glory, is exalted until self fades into insignificance.

In the Light of God's Love is one of those unusual books.

In the first chapter you will encounter the cross of Jesus with self-forgetful understanding. Riding on the beautiful wave of Calvary's love, each chapter that follows will apply the healing power of that love at the practical level of your daily Christian experience. Personal salvation, obedience, temptation, failure, and relationships—all are pondered with fresh insight in the light of God's love.

Paperback, 125 pages.   0-8163-1334-2   US$9.99

An Endless Falling in Love
Ty Gibson

A rare blend of smart and heart, *An Endless Falling in Love* is an intellectual and emotional journey into the character of God and the gift of eternity. Beyond the clichés about harps, clouds, gold streets, and gates of pearl, Gibson shows eternal life to be an ever-deepening free-fall into friendship-love with God. Against this backdrop, the doctrines of the Trinity, Creation, the Fall, the Incarnation, and the Cross, and other Bible-truths take on a beauty and lushness that will forever alter your views about salvation.

Paperback, 198 pages.   0-8163-1979-0   US$12.99

Order from your ABC by calling **1-800-765-6955,** or get online and shop our virtual store at **www.AdventistBookCenter.com.**
- Read a chapter from your favorite book
- Order online
- Sign up for e-mail notices on new products

Prices subject to change without notice